Derek Ansell was born in north London and has lived in Berkshire for the past thirty-five years. He writes regular reviews of live jazz and classical music for magazines and newspapers and has contributed more than two hundred articles and numerous interviews, record and book reviews to *Jazz Journal International*. In 1998 Citron Press published his novel *The Whitechapel Murders*, a fictional account of the notorious Jack The Ripper murders in London in 1888, and he is currently writing a novel set in London in the mid-1950s.

WORKOUT

The Music of Hank Mobley

WORKOUT

The Music of Hank Mobley

Derek Ansell

Published in 2008

Northway Publications
39 Tytherton Road, London N19 4PZ, UK.
www.northwaybooks.com

© Derek Ansell 2008

The right of Derek Ansell to be identified as author of this work has been asserted by him in accordance with the Copyright, Designs and Patents Act 1988.

All rights reserved. No part of this book may be reproduced, stored in a retrieval system or transmitted, in any form or by any means without prior permission in writing of the publisher, nor be otherwise circulated in any form of binding or cover other than that in which it is published and without a similar condition including this condition being imposed on the subsequent purchaser.

Front cover photo is of Hank Mobley at the Rudy Van Gelder Studio, Englewood Cliffs, New Jersey, on March 18th 1966 for his *A Slice of the Top* recording session. Back cover photo is of Mobley with Doug Watkins at a rehearsal for his *Hank Mobley Quartet* session in May 1955. Photos by Francis Wolff, © Mosaic Images. The publishers acknowledge with thanks the generous assistance of Michael Cuscuna. Visit *www.mosaicimages.com* for information on obtaining prints of Francis Wolff photographs.

Cover design by Adam Yeldham of Raven Design.

A CIP record for this book is available from the British Library.

ISBN 978 09550908 8 2

Printed and bound in Great Britain by Cromwell Press Ltd, Trowbridge, Wiltshire.

Contents

Acknowledgements		viii
Introduction		ix
1.	Early Messages: 1954–55	1
2.	A Leader on Records	18
3.	Unearthing the Rarities	25
4.	The Jazz Life	31
5.	Poppin' and the Curtain Call Session	38
6.	Soul Station	45
7.	Working Out	54
8.	The Turnaround	70
9.	Consolidation	89
10.	Europe	99
11.	The Enigma of Hank Mobley	118
12.	Coming Home	125
13.	A Slice of the Top	134
14.	The Last Years	140
15.	Straight No Filter	145
16.	The Legacy	152
Epilogue		159
Notes		163
Records		167
Index		171

Acknowledgements

My thanks are due to David Nathan at the National Jazz Archive at Loughton, Essex, for digging out some features on Hank Mobley from the 1960s and 1970s. These articles from *Jazz Monthly*, *Jazz Journal* and *Melody Maker* were very helpful.

The editor and staff at *DownBeat* magazine provided a copy of the one important interview Hank gave, to John Litweiler in 1973, which opened a few doors to his character and motivation. They also gave permission to quote from this interview. Simon Spillett, a tenor saxophonist who claims Mobley as one of his favourite tenor players, not only helped with permission to quote from his articles on Hank in *Jazz Journal International* in 2003 and 2004 but also, very kindly, sent me copies of tapes with music not generally available and known only to a few collectors. I have also appreciated the support of Michael Cuscuna and the staff at Mosaic Records.

My own collection of Mobley records is fairly substantial but some gaps were filled when Eddie and Janet Cook sent me new Mobley reissues to review for *Jazz Journal International*, including the rare Debut sessions now available on Jazz Door Records. Information gleaned from record sleeve notes and reviews, in particular those by John Litweiler, have all proved useful.

My sincere thanks to all concerned.

Derek Ansell

Introduction

Hank Mobley was unique. He was much admired by other musicians, many of whom rated him as one of the very greatest modern stylists, and a tenor saxophonist who sold more records than almost anybody else on the Blue Note label. Yet he still managed to attract a lot of flack, at best, from critics and jazz commentators who undervalued his solo strengths and contributions to modern jazz and, at worst, from those who regarded him as obscure and unimportant.

A jazz musician who recorded twenty-five LPs as a leader for one independent record label and more for other companies can hardly be called obscure. Add in numerous sideman appearances in the 1950s and 1960s – far more than most musicians in his sphere, and a face that was well-known from liner photographs and even made the cover shot of *The Blue Note Years: The Jazz Photography of Francis Wolff* and you have a significant musician. And yet Hank Mobley was consistently underrated, unfavourably compared with some of his more flamboyant contemporaries of the day and never really given his due as a consistently inventive and often innovative tenor sax soloist and a composer of considerable skill and imagination.

Should you wish to know more about the major jazz musicians who made their names in the 1950s and 1960s, you will find plenty of books about John Coltrane, Sonny Rollins and other key figures of the bop and hard bop movements of that time, but until now there has not been one about Hank Mobley. Why? The general consensus seems to be that Coltrane, Rollins and even lesser talents such as Johnny Griffin, possessing hard, edgy tones in the fashion of the day, all tended to overshadow Mobley's quieter approach.

The hard bop sound was certainly used and developed by those musicians and you could hardly ignore the spectacular playing of Rollins and Trane, but it really wasn't that simple, as I attempt to show over the following pages. Partly, of course, it was a question of influences: Rollins from Coleman Hawkins; Trane from Hawk and Lester Young; Stan Getz from Lester Young. Getz is a good example: tremendously popular, he developed a modern, Parker-influenced variation of Young's approach to tenor playing but, because the earlier styles and sound were so well known to jazz aficionados, he was quickly accepted and soon winning polls and filling venues. Hank Mobley, on the other hand, had a light, lyrical sound that was all his own, not like that of anybody who had gone before, even though his style descended directly from Charlie Parker.

Jazz, for all the innovation, excitement and boundary pushing by key musicians over the years has, curiously, always managed to breed ultra-conservative followers. Jazz fans tend to stick to what they know and like and take slowly, if at all, to new ideas and styles. It took a long time for most fans to adjust to the modern jazz of Charlie Parker and Dizzy Gillespie, and even longer for them to accept Thelonious Monk, that iconoclastic genius of modern piano. It took years for the innovations of Ornette Coleman, Cecil Taylor and Eric Dolphy to become absorbed into the mainstream and many jazz enthusiasts have still not made the final transition. Most jazz critics and writers cannot agree about anything much and fans tend to stick with a particular style and era to the exclusion of all else.

It is true to say that all jazz enthusiasts have a particular favourite jazz era, the one in which they first started to listen to the music. This overrides almost every other consideration for most people. I have yet to meet anyone who is exempt from this rule, myself included. Older people often have a lifelong love of New Orleans jazz that seldom extends beyond the swing era of the 1930s and early 1940s. The big band era is everything to some batches of enthusiasts and they have little time for other jazz periods. Others, including many prominent critics, embraced the bop revolution of the 1940s, happily congratulating themselves on their powers of understanding, but could never quite come to terms with the minor revolution of the 1960s avant-garde movement. Yet more are totally overwhelmed by the cool music of the West Coast school in California and have little or no time for any other style. Show me someone who embraces the best of jazz and the greatest musicians from New Orleans to California by way of Chicago and New York City, who can and does enjoy a wide range of jazz by Armstrong, Beiderbecke, Young, Hawkins, Parker, Gillespie, Monk, Coltrane, Rollins, Mobley, Coleman, Dolphy, Taylor (Cecil, that is) and many others, and you will be showing me a real jazz enthusiast, someone who understands the true, ever-changing, ever-developing, constantly evolving nature of this music. But there are precious few of them around.

Hank Mobley was just one of many who missed out on the accolades and the big time and the fame and fortune. Partly, his ultimate, overall failure to make it was his own fault; it happened for many other reasons too. This is his story.

1

Early Messages 1954–55

Hank Mobley seemed to arrive on the jazz scene in New York City from out of nowhere, with a sound and style all his own. Where others had taken years of preparation, rehearsal and work in various rhythm and blues bands, there was Hank, with little playing experience behind him, fully formed and raring to go. He was one of a relatively short list of great tenor saxophonists; innovative, creative jazz musicians who not only had a distinctive sound but contributed immensely to the development and evolution of the music.

Consider the most important musicians on the tenor saxophone. Coleman Hawkins came along first and made his mark as a distinctive soloist. For many years Hawkins was the major influence and source of inspiration to all jazz musicians who played tenor sax and the most important of them took their lead and general stylistic approach from him. Then, some years later, Lester Young showed that a radically different approach was possible. Many years after that, Sonny Rollins came along with an updated approach to the Hawkins concept and a little while later John Coltrane appeared with a sound and style that were utterly unique. Although his style had roots in what Hawkins and Young had done before, it was completely and utterly new and original. So new and original, in fact, that it took many commentators and people who thought they knew a thing or two about jazz at least ten years to appreciate the man's importance. In the 1960s, briefly, Albert Ayler offered yet another unique voice with a sound and style that were both radical and, in their reliance on old folk strains, fairly conservative.

The odd man out was Hank Mobley. He started to play with big name bands in 1951 when Max Roach hired him but, from then until his premature death in May 1986, he was creative, original, often brilliant, but consistently underrated by observers and critics of the music.

Those are the bare facts. To examine the reasons why he was so important we need to study his music. Fortunately he recorded prolifically: twenty-five albums as a leader for Blue Note between 1954 and 1970 but, after including other labels such as Prestige, Savoy and Roulette, the total is more like thirty-four. Alfred Lion, the founder of Blue Note Records, recognised the innovative skills and competence of Mobley, who soon became a leader on records. But most of the rest of his career was spent as a sideman in other people's bands and that gives us our first clue to the personality and character of Hank Mobley, the man and the musician.

* * *

Mobley was never a forceful or assertive character. We know from other musicians with whom he worked, and from observers of the jazz scene in the 1950s and 1960s, that he was always something of a recluse, going out to work in various combos and orchestras, playing his part and then returning home.

During the intervals at clubs he would disappear out to the car park or street and sit smoking in his car until it was time to play again. Writing his obituary in the September 1986 edition of *Jazz Journal*, Dave Gelly told of the time he visited the USA in 1963 and heard Hank play at the Five Spot Cafe in a combo with pianist Barry Harris. In conversation with Gelly, the pianist said: 'Don't bother trying to talk to Hank. He doesn't even talk to me. He's sitting out there in his car and he won't come in till it's time for the next set.' Harris pointed out of the window and Gelly saw a shadowy figure sitting in an old, beaten-up Buick parked at the kerbside. Like some professional actors who hide behind a part and can bellow out the lines of *King Lear* or *Henry V* on-stage and then come off and be almost inarticulate off-stage, Hank could play with the very best jazz musicians on equal terms but once off the bandstand he became quiet, reticent and very introverted. Gelly's *Jazz Journal* obituary also pointed out that Mobley's sound, live, was something to marvel at, especially for those who were sitting close to the bandstand and hearing it direct. Although the recordings for Blue Note engineered by Rudy Van Gelder were very good and he probably produced the closest thing to a natural jazz sound on records, he did have his own idiosyncratic methods, adding a little echo and, as Gelly put it, he 'boosted Mobley's volume in relation to the rest of the band . . . In person the sound shrank to a conversational level. It was laconic and somehow beady-eyed, a cool tone for a cool head.'

Van Gelder always jealously guarded the secrets of his methods of recording and the details of the equipment he used, even from fellow-professional recording engineers, so we are unlikely ever to know exactly what was added or subtracted from the natural sound of musicians such as Mobley. We can be sure, however, that the engaging, light blue gauzy sound that we hear on the best recordings was enhanced by the natural balance obtained in good clubs with light amplification; a situation that seems lost beyond recall in these days of massive over-amplified PA sound systems.

If booked to play in a band Mobley would always give his very best but if, as sometimes happened, he was distracted by another soloist, or found on arrival at the gig that another musician that he hadn't known about had been booked alongside him, he would retreat into his shell and play as little as possible, doing just enough to fulfil his obligation to the bandleader but shunning the chance to solo often, if at all.

He was, certainly, reticent and quiet most of the time, living for his music but unwilling, it seems, to take on the responsibilities of leadership. This must account, in part, for some of his early failure to attract attention or to show just how good a soloist he was, for his appearances could be limited by his own reservations and attitude. Early on in life, however, Mobley had decided that he wanted to be a musician.

* * *

He was born Henry Mobley in Eastman, Georgia, on July 7th 1930, but his parents moved to Elizabeth, New Jersey when he was still a small child. It was a musical family. Hank's grandmother was a church organist and his mother played piano. He also had an uncle who played piano and other instruments and there was always plenty of piano music about the house. At the age of eight he started taking piano lessons but he did not become serious about music until the age of sixteen, when he developed an interest in the saxophone. He managed to get a long school-holiday job in a bowling alley and saved money to buy a sax. When he had saved enough for his purchase, he was dismayed to find that the dealer had gone on holiday for a month. The young Hank was pretty single-minded and determined, however, and turned a problem to his advantage. As he told John Litweiler in his interview for *DownBeat* magazine in 1973, he got himself a music book and by the time the dealer returned had learned the whole instrument:

All I had to do was put it in my mouth and play . . . I'll tell you, when I was about eight they wanted me to play piano, but I wanted to play cops and robbers. But when I got serious the music started coming easily.[1]

At this time he was studying carpentry and auto mechanics and was, by his own admission, a nervous wreck from studying to be a machinist. Fortunately, the shop teacher was also a trumpet player and he heard Mobley play the Lester Young solo from 'One O'Clock Jump', note for note. He said to the youngster: 'There's no room out there for a black machinist. The way you play saxophone, why don't you study that?' And that is precisely what Mobley did. He left the machine shop that year and, as he told Litweiler, 'I just put on my hip clothes and went chasing women and going to rock and roll things.'

His uncle, Dave Mobley, gave him advice that he must have taken very seriously, for it helped to shape his development into a particularly individualistic tenor soloist. He recommended listening to Lester Young and then to Don Byas, Dexter Gordon and Sonny Stitt, and 'anyone who can swing and get a message across'. He also told him, 'If you're with somebody that plays loud, you play soft, if somebody plays fast, you play slow. If you try to play the same thing they're playing you're in trouble.' This advice came when Hank was just eighteen years old and he certainly took it to heart and never forgot it.

At the start of the 1950s, Mobley became a professional musician. He was already working in rhythm-and-bluesman Paul Gayten's band and, soon after that, he added a gig as a member of a Newark club's house-band, together with pianist Walter Davis Jr. The club presented weekly guest front-liners from New York, and Mobley, who must have learned fast, soon found himself supporting and playing alongside the likes of Billie Holiday, Bud Powell, Miles Davis and a host of top soloists. The need to think on his feet and the determination to take Uncle Dave's advice must have been the origin of his technique, later developed to a fine art, of making lines breathe when he wanted them to, and not when the music dictated it. He fashioned a rhythmic ability like nobody else's; his rhythmic flexibility always got him out of trouble and whatever was played, no matter how complex the line, he found ways to make everything fit for him and come out right. Good examples can be heard throughout his recordings, particularly his sterling sets in the mid to late 1950s and his masterworks in the early 1960s.

It was while Hank was working at the Newark club that Max Roach was booked to front the house-band. This was a weekend in 1951; Roach promptly offered the tenor player a job in his regular band. As Hank put it to John Litweiler:

> I was just twenty-one. We opened in a place on 125th Street in Harlem; Charlie Parker had just been there before me, and here I come. I'm scared to death – here's Sonny Rollins, Jackie McLean, Kenny Dorham, Gerry Mulligan, just about all the young musicians came by there.

Scared he may have been, thrown into the deep end by Roach's recognition of an unformed but vital musical talent, but he soon became accepted on the New York scene and, unlike most musicians before him, he did not have to make the agonising decision of moving alone to NYC and taking his chances with all the competition. He had been taken there from Newark by a major leader with a ready-made gig lined up. Soon Mobley was working regularly in NYC clubs and Roach recorded 'Mobleyzation', his first composition. By the time the combo broke up, Mobley was already established and never short of work. It was during this period in the early 1950s that he was called on by bassist Oscar Pettiford, who recruited for Duke at that time, to sub in the Duke Ellington Orchestra for two weeks. 'Jimmy Hamilton had to have some dental work done,' Hank recalled in 1973. 'I didn't play clarinet but I played some of the clarinet parts on tenor.' Mobley remembered hanging out with Paul Gonsalves, Willie Cook and Ray Nance. 'We were the four horsemen, but nobody would show me the music and it was all messed up. So Duke would say, "A Train", and while I was fumbling for the music the band had started. Finally Harry Carney and Cat Anderson helped me straighten it out.'

There was plenty of work for the young saxophonist. He worked the clubs and studios of NYC, took part in a second tour with Paul Gayten's band and in the summer of 1953 was with Clifford Brown in Tadd Dameron's band at the Club Harlem in Atlantic City. Meantime, Max Roach, then in California, was looking for really good musicians for a new, all-star quintet. He tried to reach Mobley by telephone but was unable to locate him. He did make contact with Clifford Brown and so history was made with the beginning of the Clifford Brown–Max Roach Quintet. Had the drummer managed to find Hank, he might have been the tenor player with the group rather than Harold Land and later, briefly, Sonny Rollins. Instead, Mobley joined up with Dizzy Gillespie and played in the trumpeter's big band for a time. That lasted for a year and then there was a new turning point in his career when he joined pianist Horace Silver.

Silver had a quartet with an engagement at Minton's Playhouse, one of the places where bebop, or modern jazz, was first played. He had Doug Watkins on bass, Arthur Edgehill on drums and in 1954 Mobley became his front-line soloist on tenor saxophone. As Hank told Litweiler, 'On weekends Art Blakey and Kenny Dorham would come in to jam, 'cause they were right round the corner.'

This was the beginning of a new and superb quintet, which would become the Jazz Messengers, the first of a series of bands with this name but with ever-changing personnel, and it would go on into the 1980s under the leadership of drummer Art Blakey. But in the beginning it was a cooperative unit and had no name. Horace Silver was the best-known musician at the time and the first studio recordings, originally released as two ten-inch LPs and later combined into a twelve-inch, for Blue Note, were billed as Horace Silver and the Jazz Messengers. The cooperative that grew out of the Minton's engagement consisted of Dorham, Mobley, Silver, Watkins and Edgehill. They would use their individual names to get gigs and as soon as one of them landed a job, he would contact the others and they would all play. After a time Edgehill dropped out and Blakey became the cooperative drummer on a regular basis. Mobley said: 'Horace'd get a job, or Art or Kenny would get a job; we'd split the money equally; I think that's where the cooperative started.'

On November 13th 1954, the first sessions were recorded for Blue Note of what became arguably the best single recording by the original Jazz Messengers. The title of the two ten-inch LPs was *Horace Silver and the Jazz Messengers* and the music recorded then and at the second session on February 6th 1955 marked the start of the most famous academy of hard bop ever. The Jazz Messengers lasted through four decades and only expired on the death of their leader Art Blakey. But in 1954 the band was very much an equal shares cooperative, nominally led by the pianist, and their first, and arguably their best-ever tenor saxophonist, was the young, up and coming Hank Mobley.

It was at this point that Mobley should have become reasonably well known and appreciated but recognition and praise for his playing were slow to arrive. The LP *Horace Silver and the Jazz Messengers*, when it was eventually released as a twelve-inch album, drew praise for Silver, Dorham and the rhythm section but most commentators singled out Mobley as the weakest member of the combo. Perhaps it was due to his relaxed sound and unique manner of phrasing. Although Hank's style was unformed in those early days he still managed to sound like nobody else but himself. His unusual way with rhythm was unexpected and his stylistic influence, such as could be detected, was directly from Charlie Parker, while at the time, virtually all tenor saxophonists were playing like Lester Young or Stan Getz. Only the very young Sonny Rollins was beginning to make a stir with a more robust sound that was, in effect, a modern variation of Coleman Hawkins filtered through the innovations of Charlie Parker. Right from the beginning, Mobley was a soloist who ploughed his own furrow and virtually ignored what was being played by other musicians on his instrument.

Horace Silver and the Jazz Messengers established Silver as a combo leader and composer; he had written all the material except for Mobley's 'Hankering'. The quintet worked successfully for about a year and a half as the Jazz Messengers and as a cooperative unit. Long before their time together ended, however, Blakey had begun gradually to assert himself as the unofficial leader and it is his voice that is heard making all the announcements on the excellent two-CD set *The Jazz Messengers at the Café Bohemia*, recorded on November 23rd 1955.

Hank's technical proficiency was already assured by the time he recorded with the first Messengers group in 1954–55. His tenor sax floats out of the ensemble on 'Stop Time' as easily and naturally as Lester Young's with Basie in the 1930s, but the sound is not the same. Where the vast majority of tenor players of the time sounded like Lester, Mobley already had his own thing developing. To put it as simply as possible, his sound was softer and rounder than that of the hard boppers, but harder and more resonant than Stan Getz, Richie Kamuca, Bill Perkins, Zoot Sims and the rest of Young's stylistic descendants. And his lines were Parker-inspired hard bop, albeit with a unique and, many would say, idiosyncratic attitude towards rhythm. He would cut across bar lines and somehow squeeze as many notes as he wanted into a given sequence and always make it come out sounding right or, at least, right for him.

On the liner notes to *Poppin'*, a 1957 recording first released on LP in 1980, Larry Kart described Mobley's tone as 'a sound of feline obliqueness – as soft, at times, as Stan Getz's but blue grey, like a perpetually impending rain cloud'.[2] It is a good description and one that holds for a lot of Mobley recordings. It was also Larry Kart who first pointed out, on those same liner notes, that, on the Miles Davis composition 'Tune Up':

> The apparently simple but tricky changes pretty much defeat Art Farmer and Pepper Adams; but Mobley glides through them easily, creating a line that breathes when he wants it to, not when the harmonic pattern says 'stop'.

It was this quality above all others that set Mobley apart and made him a true innovator, a musician who, like Young, Parker, Coltrane, Coleman and a very few others, made his own rules and placed his musical statements in the slots he created for them, whether they fitted the rules of music or not. One of his best early solos on *Horace Silver and the Jazz Messengers* can be heard on 'Creepin' In', a slow atmospheric piece in a minor key which has all the quintet members stretching out luxuriously.

A few weeks after *Horace Silver and the Jazz Messengers* was recorded, Hank had the opportunity to make his first LP as a leader. On March 27th 1955 he recorded *The Hank Mobley Quartet*, a ten-inch record on which he used his colleagues from the Messengers except for Kenny Dorham. As early as this, it is noticeable that Mobley was a gifted composer and all except Cole Porter's 'Love for Sale' are the saxophonist's originals. 'Hank's Prank' is a well-constructed 'I Got Rhythm' variation which features complex, lively solo work from the leader and a strong Silver statement. It is immediately apparent that these are not mere frameworks for soloists to blow on; they are fascinating original compositions, particularly 'My Sin', a yearning slow ballad, and the delightful minor opus 'Just Coolin''. Such was Mobley's ability as a composer that he would often put new compositions together in the studio, in the course of a recording session.

This LP was, according to Hank himself, his best early recording and, as noted by Bob Blumenthal on the liner notes to the Mosaic six-CD set of the saxophonist's 1950s leader dates:

> significant preparation had preceded the actual visit to Van Gelder's studio. The command of his instrument, his invention and attractive lines such as 'Walkin' the Fence', 'Avila and Tequila', and the ripe melody of 'My Sin' all combine to suggest a very well-rounded modern jazz musician as early as 1955.[3]

If I had access to a time machine, my first port of call would be the Café Bohemia on the night of November 23rd 1955. By this time, the original Jazz Messengers quintet had been recording and playing live dates regularly and had shaken down to one of the very best modern jazz combos around. Alfred Lion recorded the band for Blue Note with his regular recording engineer, Rudy Van Gelder. Portable equipment was set up in the club and it recorded just about every note played by the band on that evening. Mobley was in great form, as he often was by this time, and so too were Dorham, Silver, Watkins and the irrepressible Blakey.

With the passage of years it now seems a little strange hearing again Blakey's opening announcements from the Bohemia stage, especially when he mentions 'one of the youngest and finest bass players on the scene: Doug Watkins', and later, 'a new star on the modern jazz scene, Hank Mobley'. Hank was just twenty-five at that gig and Watkins, a superb bass player destined to die tragically young in a car crash seven years later, just twenty-one. But there can be no argument with Blakey's assertion that they were 'having a cooking session here tonight, putting the pot on in here'.

Some of the very finest hard bop ever recorded can be heard on the two volumes of *The Jazz Messengers at the Café Bohemia*. Indeed it was some of the very first hard bop, following the earlier *Art Blakey Quintet*, recorded at Birdland in February 1954. This set is a further refinement of the style created simultaneously by Blakey working with Clifford Brown and Lou Donaldson, and by Max Roach, who was also working with trumpeter Clifford Brown. If the Birdland set with Brown was a statement of intent, full of fire and fury, headlong tempos and relentless swing and some gorgeous lyricism – a virtual definition of the new hard bop – then the Café Bohemia sets are a consolidation; there is a feeling of control and almost of relaxation throughout these performances. It is as if Blakey and company are telling us that the new music is often hard and fast and furious but it is also warm, melodic and lyrical. Only the uncompromising approach and the near equal status of the rhythm section to the front line has changed and changed for ever. Few rhythm sections would be shrinking violets, content to provide a soft-focus, light beat in the background, after these recordings were heard and noted.

The major difference between bop and hard bop was in the stripping down to the basic essentials of the music and the aggression of the latter, and in the greater role overall played by piano, bass and drums. The style, as initiated by the first Messengers in 1954–55, also called for great rhythmic diversity and the ability of the front-line instruments to swing hard at all tempi. It was here that Mobley was crucial, not just to the original Messengers but to the entire, unfolding, hard bop movement. He could play hard and fast but also with great warmth and authority on ballads and his sound was nicely balanced between the old-style Lester Young lightness and the emerging hard sound as personified by Rollins and, a short time later, Johnny Griffin and John Coltrane. His rhythmic prowess was often unorthodox but whatever he did, however many notes he squeezed or subtracted or lengthened in the process, he always managed to swing like crazy. And that was precisely what the new style required.

The best overall picture of Mobley's emerging style and command of the hard bop genre can be gained by listening closely to all the music on these two extended-length CDs. It is all played to a very high standard and although the piano at the Bohemia always sounded 'on the edge', and about to go out of tune any minute, the ambience of the club on that night is captured to perfection and, more importantly, so is the music. Rudy Van Gelder's recording, as early as 1955, is clear and bright and each instrument can be heard to advantage in both solo and ensemble. You can also sense, if not hear, Mobley's discomfort as Art Blakey virtually forces him to come up to the microphone to announce his solo feature 'Alone Together' to the audience. But he does it, slowly, haltingly and nervously and then proceeds to play a gloriously warm and personal version of the standard.

Perhaps for historical reasons, there has been a tendency, over the years, to heap praise on the two Birdland discs by Blakey's quintet in 1954 and the studio sessions of 1954–55 that produced *Horace Silver and the Jazz Messengers*. Although Alyn Shipton praises the two Bohemia discs,[4] they are rarely heralded as essential or special recordings by jazz commentators. Personally, I have always found the Café Bohemia recordings more satisfying than, and also superior to, the other sets. It may be partly due to the ambience in the club or the audience's obvious enjoyment but most of all, I suspect, it is the immediacy and inspiration of the musicians on a night when they were all 'hot', and at their very best in all respects. And contrary to the words of some commentators (Richard Cook and Brain Morton describe Mobley on these recordings as 'a somewhat unfocused stylist'[5]), Mobley's technical facility and invention were at a consistently high level all through this long evening of music at the Bohemia.

In the liner notes for the 2001 version of the Bohemia sets, remastered by Van Gelder, Bob Blumenthal quotes Horace Silver on the front line of Kenny Dorham and Mobley: 'That horn section was so hip, you know, they were super hip. The way they phrased, and the lines they played, their harmonic knowledge was so beautiful.'[6] Careful study of these discs will also reveal that there is more variety and experimentation in Mobley's playing than on any other recordings by him at this time. If there had been any deficiencies in his playing or technical hang-ups prior to the night of November 23rd 1955, they are all resolved very inventively on the Bohemia bandstand. It was, I suggest, from this night onwards, that Hank Mobley was a force on the tenor saxophone and an important player in the evolving modern jazz scene.

After the Bohemia date Kenny Dorham left the original Messengers to start his own group, the Jazz Prophets. It was like a variation of the Messengers but, perhaps because the public was not ready for two similar-sounding bands in those days, it was short-lived. Meantime the cooperative Messengers recruited the up and coming trumpeter Donald Byrd and headed for Boston. No doubt working at a local club in the area, they headed for Harvard Square, Cambridge, on December 2nd to record *Byrd's Eye View* for the short-lived Boston-based Transition label. Donald Byrd was the leader but the band was the Jazz Messengers with local trumpeter Joe Gordon added to the line-up.

* * *

It is fortunate indeed that the vast majority of Hank Mobley's recordings were taped for Blue Note, a company that encouraged and sustained his recording career from the very beginning. It was natural enough, given his reticent temperament, that Mobley would function perfectly in the recording studio as a leader, where the responsibility for that status ended the minute the tape stopped rolling and the musicians packed up to leave.

In the early days he recorded for Prestige and Savoy, the other two leading jazz independents on the East Coast. But no preparation or rehearsal time was allowed with them; musicians had to plan music at their own expense or not at all and consequently most of the music heard on those labels sticks to basic blues or 'I Got Rhythm' variations. Blue Note was different. Recording all their sessions was Rudy Van Gelder, first in a room set up at his parents' home in Hackensack, New Jersey and, from 1959 onwards, at a custom-made recording facility he had built at Englewood Cliffs, also in New Jersey. Talking to John Litweiler, Mobley happily recalled the Blue Note recordings set up in the 1950s and 1960s:

> Savoy recorded on Fridays, Prestige on Saturdays, Blue Note on Sundays, something like that. They'd buy the whiskey and brandy Saturday night and the food on Sunday – they'd set out salami, liverwurst, bologna, rye bread, the whole bit. Only Blue Note did it; the others were a little stiff. If we had a date Sunday, I'd rehearse the band Tuesday and Thursday in a New York studio.

Blue Note had been formed in 1939 by two German immigrants, Alfred Lion and Francis Wolff. They had always recorded what they considered the best of the current contemporary scene, so in the early days had produced fine records by people such as pianist Albert Ammons, soprano saxophonist Sidney Bechet and clarinettist Edmond Hall, along with many good but lesser-known musicians. In the 1940s they gave early recording opportunities to Thelonious Monk, then somewhat neglected by jazz recording industry executives, who regarded him as too eccentric. Fats Navarro, Bud Powell and the very young Sonny Rollins also received recording dates. By the mid-1950s Blue Note were the first to record the emerging hard bop of the day as pioneered initially by Art Blakey, Horace Silver, Clifford Brown and, a little later, they recorded Hank Mobley and Kenny Dorham. It was the perfect environment for Mobley, who recorded nine LPs in the period from 1955 to 1958, although not all of them were issued at the time. He became virtually house tenor saxophonist at Blue Note and appeared on more records for the company than any other musician, with the possible exception of organist Jimmy Smith.

Perhaps most important of all, for a musician as sensitive and quiet as Hank, the atmosphere and general ambience of the Van Gelder studios and the enthusiasm of Lion and Wolff ultimately provided the ideal environment. Hank recalled in 1973 some of those record dates, remembering that at times his horn would squeak and Francis Wolff would call out in horror, 'Hank Mobley, you squeaked, you squeaked!' Mobley remembered fondly that this would cause the band to break up laughing and they couldn't get back to playing the tune. And Alfred Lion would be walking around snapping his fingers and saying, in his German-accented English: 'Mmmn,' (snap) 'Ooh!' (snap) 'Now vait a minute, it don't swing, it don't sving.' So the musicians would laugh and do it again, a little slower, and Lion would smile and say (snap), 'Fine, fine, dot really svings, ja.'

If the outside world was a cruel and unaccommodating place then, as now, and Mobley lacked the organisational abilities and strength of will to be a bandleader on the road, he found the ideal solution as a leader on record dates for Blue Note in the comfort and the user-friendly environment of both of Van

Gelder's New Jersey recording studios. But in 1955 all this was in the future. Nobody knew that Hank would remain a perpetual sideman out on the street and one of the most prolific leaders in the recording studios. All that was known then was that a new and exciting tenor saxophonist was emerging and showing great promise.

2

A Leader on Records

Paradoxically, Hank Mobley came closest to being a leader right at the start of his career, during the time when the original Jazz Messengers were an active unit, from late 1954 to mid-1956. The band really did work as a cooperative combo with decisions being made only if every member of the team was happy about them. But Art Blakey, a natural leader who had led earlier bands, notably the sterling quintet he took into Birdland and recorded in February 1954, began to assert himself and to make the announcements, as the recorded sets at the Bohemia attest. And the complicated five-equal-musicians set-up was difficult to implement and maintain: it carried the seeds of its own destruction in having three musicians, Dorham, Silver and Blakey, who were all leaders or potential leaders. But for those months of 1955 and part of 1956, the band toured and played gigs at schools, colleges and clubs and was constantly on the road. Mobley was an integral part of the group and could make decisions along with the other four men about where they played and, in theory at least, what they played and who took solos on certain features.

In spite of the regular live dates, Hank still managed to find time to record ten LPs for Prestige, Savoy and Blue Note during 1956. It was a phenomenal output and the music was of a uniformly high standard on all of them. The most unusual album was *Tenor Conclave*, where he found himself in a four-tenor line-up with Zoot Sims, Al Cohn and John Coltrane although, in those days, Coltrane was just another good tenor saxist who was beginning to be noticed and to make a name for himself with the exciting Miles Davis Quintet. On the blues, 'Tenor Conclave' and 'Bob's Boys', it is, surprisingly, Mobley who sounds most laid-back and his choruses have a casual, apparently effortless feel to them. It all just flows naturally: the sometimes complex but uncontrived rhythmic patterns, the soft, round sound ('a round sound' was his own description to differentiate between the hard sound of the ultra-hard boppers and the soft-focus tone of the Lester Young followers) and the constantly inventive melodic patterns that each of his solos contained.

Two of the leading men from the Lester-influenced school are on the record with him but, well as Sims and Cohn play, it is Mobley and Coltrane who manage to sound most relaxed and inventive throughout. An example of this is 'How Deep is the Ocean', a standard that plays for fifteen minutes and gives everybody a chance to stretch out. It is remarkable for the sheer ease with which Hank blows his choruses and how sophisticated they sound in this context. This was, after all, just a hastily assembled blowing session. The founder of the Prestige label, Bob Weinstock, would never countenance paying for rehearsals and so it is rare to find a Prestige disc from this era with anything other than variations on the blues, standard songs or popular variations of 'I Got Rhythm' chord changes.

* * *

Mobley always expressed satisfaction with his first LP as a leader (*The Hank Mobley Quartet*), saying that he thought it was the best of his early recordings and indicating that considerable preparation had been carried out before going into the studio. Although he would later become a regular feature at Blue Note, it was not until November 25th 1956 that he made his second LP as bandleader for the company. That was one year and eight months after his first album, made on March 27th 1955. In between he had been busy cutting items such as *The Jazz Message of Hank Mobley Volume One* and *Volume Two* for Savoy Records and *Mobley's Message* and *Mobley's Second Message* for Prestige. As all three record companies were based close to each other in New York and all used the same recording engineer, Rudy Van Gelder, it probably all felt very similar to Hank, whichever company he was recording for.

After the break-up of the original Jazz Messengers, Horace Silver tired of the cooperative format and decided to form his own quintet, taking Byrd, Watkins and Mobley with him, and leaving Blakey with just the name and the task of forming an entirely new band. If that sounds sudden, premeditated and harsh on Blakey, the sleeve note to *Horace Silver and the Jazz Messengers*[1] suggests that the main reason for the instantaneous break-up of the Messengers was a record date for Columbia in 1956 for which, even though Blakey was paid as leader, he never got around to paying any of the other musicians.

Hank had a regular gig with Horace and plenty of time to record on the many occasions that they were based in New York City. In due course, however, a relationship began to build up between the saxophonist and Blue Note partners Alfred Lion and Francis Wolff which was to determine his future recording career. Because they admired his work so much, even though virtually all the jazz critics were either ignoring or deriding him, they began to put him in the studio more times than almost any other musician.

On 25th November 1956, however, it was just another record date by another promising tenor man whom the Blue Note partners happened to think was a bit special. Perhaps to place him firmly in the spotlight and make him look like the tenor man of the moment, they engaged both Donald Byrd and Lee Morgan on trumpets to share the front line with him. Byrd was, at that time, the most prominent and, many thought, the most promising hard bop trumpeter since Clifford Brown, who had died in a car crash on June 26th of that year. Lee Morgan, who had caused a sensation in the Dizzy Gillespie Orchestra, playing solo on Diz's usual feature 'A Night in Tunisia', was beginning to be seen as the next great hard bop trumpet soloist and recorded his first LP for Blue Note in 1956. These two, along with a sterling rhythm section, featuring old pal Horace Silver, bassist Paul Chambers and drummer Charli Persip, would set Hank up for a sizzling session. Certainly titles like 'Touch and Go' have all the hallmarks of the best hard bop of the period: driving rhythm coordinated by Silver's slashing, percussive approach and high-octane trumpet solos from both stylists that fairly burn the paint off the walls at times. Into this hard bop cauldron of fire and brimstone, Mobley's tenor comes floating, almost casually and nonchalantly refusing to be baited by the stratospheric leaps of the trumpets and the driving rhythm section. The contrast is remarkably effective, as indeed were all Mobley's pairings with other front-line horn players.

According to the original liner notes of the first issued LP (*Hank Mobley Sextet with Donald Byrd and Lee Morgan*), the two-trumpet front line was Mobley's idea. Whether he also suggested Donald Byrd and Lee Morgan is open to speculation, but expanding on his idea for the two brass instruments, Leonard Feather's original liner notes quote Hank as explaining: 'It gave us a limited range, and it was a challenge to make the writing interesting. We used a certain amount of closed voicing, some unison lines, some double thirds; I think the ensemble got a good blend.'

It certainly did. Not for the first time and certainly not the last, Mobley proved that he was adept at writing material and arrangements, on the spot, in the recording studio if necessary. In the liner essay for the Mosaic box of Mobley's 1950s dates, annotator Bob Blumenthal suggests that 'Touch and Go' from this session offers a good illustration of how Mobley could make a simple idea interesting.

> The sixteen-bar theme is equally divided between suspension and swing, with further drama provided by the fanfare built around Persip's drums at the opening and close. Everyone gets a solo (Chambers bows his) with a slightly overeager Morgan taking the first trumpet spot. The youngster would attain more polish quickly, though his energy and brash ideas are already present. Mobley eases into the tenor solo, then starts dealing quickly; his contrasting of simple and complex ideas is exemplary, and his tone is indeed round.[2]

It is also a fragmented and highly unorthodox solo as modern jazz solos go, but I will expand on this point in a later chapter. The key words in Blumenthal's description of that particular track are 'Mobley eases into the tenor solo.' As if constantly seeking tension and release in all his music, Hank always eased gently into tenor solos no matter how ferocious the onslaught from the previous trumpet, trombone or other saxophone had been. Morgan, a brilliant if often erratic soloist in the early days, was an ideal foil for Mobley and over the years they frequently linked up on record and NYC club gigs. But if the November 25th sextet session was a typically abrasive and swinging hard bop set, Hank's next LP was not.

* * *

Early in January 1957, Hank went into the Van Gelder studio in Hackensack to record *Hank Mobley and His All Stars*, which Bob Blumenthal describes in his Mosaic notes as one of the high points in the Mobley discography. It is certainly that, as well as being one of the most relaxed and naturally easy-swinging sessions of the mid-1950s hard bop era. Featuring Milt Jackson on vibes, sharing the front line with Hank's tenor and the original Messengers' rhythm section of Silver, Watkins and Blakey, it even justifies the 'All Stars' tag.

The music on this LP was perhaps the first indication of the mature Mobley, a man emerging from the status of jobbing tenor saxophonist to accomplished soloist, composer and leader. Had he been a more gregarious, outgoing personality, there is little doubt that Mobley would eventually have emerged as a top-class bandleader and toured with some of the most intriguing bands ever heard in jazz. All the tracks on this LP are Mobley originals and all are attractive themes, much more than the usual slim sketch of melody used as a launching pad for solos that passed for much of the jazz of the 1940s and 1950s. Pride of place on the disc must go to 'Lower Stratosphere', which has all the hallmarks of a superior twelve-bar blues. As Blumenthal points out, Mobley does not set this one up with the usual couple of walking choruses from bassist Watkins but instead has the bass playing pedal point for an eight-bar melody repeated twice: 'once by tenor with vibes commentary and then the other way round'.

The solos of Mobley and Jackson on this selection and, to a slightly lesser extent, on the rest of the album, are superb, riding on a smooth cushion from the rhythm section. 'Mobley's Musings', the final, slow ballad on the original LP issue, is almost as good as the blues described above. The combination of Mobley's smoky, filtered blue tenor, and Jackson's crisp, metallic vibes makes this a haunting, unique set of performances. Jackson, on loan from another record company for this album, was using an unfamiliar set of vibes, so the sound he produces here is different from any of his other recordings. Add that streamlined rhythm team that knew Hank so well, which could furnish the ideal support for everything he tried out, and you have Mobley's very best recording of the 1950s. He was to surpass this disc in 1960 and 1961 but, when this LP first came out, it is surprising that it did not cause much more of a stir in critical circles than it did. Perhaps jazz critics generally in those days were really quite conservative and did not expect, or really want, to hear anything that departed from the normal, run-of-the-mill jazz sessions of the day. This LP shows that, as early as January 13th 1957, Mobley was producing fresh, innovative jazz to a very high standard in excellent company. The trouble was that only a few people noticed and hardly anybody was listening.

3

Unearthing the Rarities

Because jazz LPs used to sell in the shops for a short period of time and then disappear without trace for decades, it is easy to overlook some of the rarer, and often superior, music recorded by musicians such as Mobley. A good case that proves this point is the output of Transition Records, a company in Boston that flourished for about three years from 1954 to 1957 and, because none of their records really sold well, then folded and died. The owner, Tom Wilson, sold the master tapes of several of his sessions to Alfred Lion of Blue Note in 1958 and, indeed, many Transition sessions were similar to those of Blue Note records: they combined the same musicians and even their cover art was very much the same, probably the result of Wilson copying the innovative style of Blue Note designers Tom Hannan and Reid Miles and photographer Francis Wolff. Although Wilson went on to work for United Artists and then Columbia, which later became part of Sony, his first instinctive efforts were among his very best. Even though Alfred Lion never got around to issuing any of the Transition material, all of it eventually saw the light of day, long after he had departed, on the label he founded. Transition Records produced some of the most intriguing and rare Hank Mobley that, over the years, only a few people got to hear.

Out of print until recently, or available only as expensive Japanese imports, were two Transition LPs featuring fascinating Hank Mobley solos: Donald Byrd's *Byrd's Eye View*, and *Watkins at Large*, the first of only two LPs by bassist Doug Watkins as a leader. Fortunately both of these sessions in full, together with another Donald Byrd Quartet album from the same period, have been released on a double Blue Note CD, Donald Byrd–Doug Watkins: *The Transition Sessions*. 'Doug's Blues', the first track of *Byrd's Eye View*, with a walking bass introduction, sounds just like the Messengers as they were at the Café Bohemia, except that Byrd has replaced Dorham on trumpet and trumpeter Joe Gordon has been added to the front line.

As nominal leader on this set, Byrd gets a good measure of the solo space, as might be expected, but laid-back tenor solos come floating out of the ensemble frequently on the two compositions Mobley wrote and again on the opening blues and the slow ballad, 'Everything Happens to Me'. Hank's solo here is so fresh and personal that, like Charlie Parker before him, he practically recomposes the familiar melody. Byrd sticks close to the original tune but Hank, as usual, is doing his own thing. This LP was made only nine days after the engagement at the Café Bohemia, and the Messengers, with their new trumpet player, were most likely in Boston for a nightclub engagement when they recorded for Transition. Because so very little was recorded by the original Messengers with Mobley, it is instructive to hear the music he recorded for Transition as both sessions are similar in style and personnel to the cooperative unit.

Hank's two originals for the *Byrd's Eye View* LP are attractive lines, reportedly composed by him in the studio, that allow for constructive solo blowing by Mobley, Byrd and, in the case of

'Hank's Tune', Joe Gordon. Mobley's solos on this and 'Hank's Other Tune' are full of surprising twists and turns, melodic invention at a brisk tempo and – his trademark – rhythmic ingenuity.

December 8th 1956 was the scheduled date for bassist Doug Watkins to go into the recording studio to make his first LP as a leader. He took with him colleagues from the Messengers, Mobley and Byrd, as well as Duke Jordan, a natural, spontaneously creative but sadly underrated pianist, guitarist Kenny Burrell and drummer Art Taylor. According to Michael Cuscuna's liner notes for *The Transition Sessions*, Watkins also brought in a seven-foot Italian bass he had just purchased. The set begins with 'Return to Paradise', a Dmitri Tiomkin tune, now almost forgotten, that kicks off with a Byrd trumpet solo and then a relaxed workout by Mobley. He moves into double time with ease and constructs a flowing solo that rides well on the dynamic but smooth pulse provided by the rhythm section. Solos by Byrd, again, and Burrell follow and the piece has that laid-back, natural swing that characterised the music of the original Messengers at this time. Duke Jordan's personal piano sound is then heard in solo and, finally, the leader's rich, woody-sounding bass, warm and resonant in a pizzicato solo, shadowed and enhanced by Taylor's sympathetic backing. Guitarist Burrell contributed 'Phinupi', the next selection, a composition he was to return to in the 1960s on a Blue Note date with tenor saxophonist Tina Brooks and Art Blakey. A composition by Thad Jones and one by Jordan offer a balanced and diverse programme of music where Mobley is on top form throughout, each solo sailing along effortlessly on that streamlined rhythm section. There is also a muscular, improvised twelve-bar blues put together in the studio, 'Phil T. McNasty's Blues', inspired, according to Horace Silver, by a character Watkins claimed to have met in a Detroit hotel bar.

With so much Mobley on record for the leading independents at this period it is very easy to miss little gems like *Byrd's Eye View* and *Watkins at Large*, but now that the three Byrd and Watkins sessions are available on a two-CD set, the music is available to all who wish to hear it. And it is of equal quality to the more familiar Blue Note, Savoy and Prestige releases.

Even more rare and esoteric – although the music was much more basic – were the early recordings that Mobley made towards the end of the time he spent working in drummer Max Roach's group. Over the years since they were recorded for Charles Mingus' short-lived Debut label, these very early examples of Hank's tenor sax have been extremely difficult to come by in the UK unless you were able to get hold of the expensive limited-edition Japanese imports that surfaced occasionally. In 2003, however, a CD appeared on the Jazz Factory label, *Hank Mobley: The Complete Jazz Message Sessions with Kenny Clarke*, which offered all of Mobley's 1956 titles recorded with drummer Kenny Clarke for the Savoy label plus the rarely heard April 10th 1953 and April 21st 1953 Debut titles.

The first four tracks, which include versions of 'Mobleyzation', one of Mobley's earliest compositions, and the popular song of the period 'Glow Worm', feature Idrees Sulieman and Leon Comegys on trumpets, Gigi Gryce on alto sax and Walter Davis Jr, who worked with Hank in New Jersey, on piano. These pieces are tightly structured bop readings of two compositions by Hank, one by leader Roach and one popular song. Mobley's first solo on 'Orientation' finds him sounding somewhat like early Sonny Rollins. He gets more into his stride with his 'Mobleyzation' line, which is an indication of things to come. The elements of relaxed swing and audacious rhythmic placements are already evident and the sound is beginning to take on a personal flavour. 'Glow Worm' is a banal melody and Gryce's solo seems to reflect the fact that he is not happy playing it. 'Sfax' by Roach is better, a typical bop-type theme with plenty of space for the drummer's flamboyant solo style.

Of far more interest to Mobley fans, though, are the six tracks recorded on April 21st 1953 in New York where Mobley is the only front-line soloist in a quartet with Walter Davis, Franklin Skeete on bass and the leader, Max Roach, on drums. Hank meets the lightning tempo of 'Just One of Those Things' comfortably and his snaking solo is always intriguing as he shares the spotlight duties with his leader. The floating tenor sound of the early Blue Note years is already beginning to shape up on these sides with 'Cou Manchi-Cou' being a good example. Following on are 'Kismet' and then Hank demonstrating that he was already acting on his uncle's advice to be different as he takes a slow and leisurely approach to Charlie Parker's blues 'Chi Chi'. This must have sounded ultra-cool to the heavy boppers of the early 1950s, with Hank sailing through his choruses and sounding very comfortable with the theme and Roach's easy-sounding but thrusting rhythmic work behind him.

Best of all, however, is 'I'm a Fool to Want You', which gives an early indication that Mobley would soon become a consummate performer and interpreter of slow ballads. This reading is warm and breathy, faintly reminiscent of Lester Young and Ben Webster at their lyrical best but already indicating trademark Mobley methods of individualistic phrasing and expression. It is a fine performance with tenor sax front and centre throughout and again makes me wish that Hank had managed to fulfil his ambition to record a whole album of ballads.

Anybody who already has the Savoy material may feel that this Jazz Factory CD is not worth buying, but it may be recommended for the ten rare tracks with Max Roach. The music has been digitally remastered to twenty-four-bit resolution, processed using the Sonic Solutions noise-reduction system and mastered to CD using Prism SMS noise shaping, and so the music is presented with great clarity, sounding as good as is possible with fifty-year-old material. Generally speaking, they have succeeded in capturing Mobley's warm, resonant tone fairly faithfully, particularly on the Savoy sides, which were originally engineered by Rudy Van Gelder. The Debut material also sounds clean and reasonably bright. These previously rare and unique sessions on the Jazz Factory CD *Hank Mobley: The Complete Jazz Message Sessions with Kenny Clarke* are worth acquiring for early Mobley and some first-rate early hard bop but, in terms of musical quality, *The Transition Sessions* album is superior and is recommended without reservation.

4

The Jazz Life

The trials and tribulations of the jazz life are always a danger to the sensitive musician, and more so in the 1950s than today. The culture then dictated – wrongly of course – that if Charlie Parker as a heroin addict could play the way he did when high on drugs, every other gifted musician could play better on than off. It seems not to have mattered how many times Parker, unable to get off himself, cautioned musicians and everybody else to stay away from drugs and indicated that nobody ever played better when using heroin: the message did not get across. During the middle part of the 1950s Hank Mobley was not troubled by drugs. The irony of the situation was that he often used to help out Sonny Rollins who, at that time, was hooked. He told John Litweiler in 1973: 'In the early days Sonny Rollins used to have a few problems and I was kind of cool, so every time he'd have a problem they'd come and hire me.'[1] Rollins later straightened himself out and never looked back, but at that time his situation and Hank's were the reverse of the way things were in later years.

The next Blue Note recording under Mobley's leadership was *The Hank Mobley Quintet*, recorded at the Van Gelder studios in Hackensack on March 8th 1957. The band is, to all intents and purposes, the original Jazz Messengers with Art Farmer substituting for Kenny Dorham. On the original LP, sleeve note annotator Robert Levin gives an example of the jazz life and the sort of things that can happen on the road. He recalls a rainy Friday night in December 1956 when the Messengers had been booked to play a concert at the Far Rockaway High School in Long Island. The purpose had been to educate the students, aged from fourteen to eighteen, in good jazz. Harry Colomby, who taught American History at the school, had booked the band for an 8.30 pm start but at 8.45 he was still standing outside the premises, looking at the heavy rain, as a pick-up rock 'n' roll band opened the show instead. Eventually, as Levin put it: 'the headlights of a black sedan pierced the misty night air and Colomby uncrossed his half frozen fingers. The Jazz Messengers had arrived.'[2]

It transpired that the band had been playing at the Storyville Club in Boston and had then driven from there to the Long Island gig, a long journey in bad weather that had proved hazardous; during its course Watkins' bass had been damaged. The band had spent considerable time locating another bass and then continued, suffering further frustration with the difficulty of finding the school after a long and tiring journey. Of course the end of the story is upbeat, proving once again the resilience and good intentions of major jazz musicians. Upon their arrival, Mobley, Dorham and company went straight onstage after a short introduction and played a stirring set. Levin also pointed out that the concert was paid for by the school and so the rates couldn't have been much more than scale. Even so they had played on that night with enthusiasm, vigour and with the sort of enjoyment usually reserved for after-hours sessions with friends.

That is just one story recalled by a jazz critic of a particular evening when several things had gone wrong, but you could multiply and magnify that event several times over and still never get close to the regular trials and tribulations of the working jazz musician in the mid-1950s.

The *Hank Mobley Quintet* recording session proved to be the last to feature the wonderfully rich and resilient rhythm section of Silver, Watkins and Blakey. Almost as though Blue Note sensed this, the company produced a striking cover for the LP with a great photograph of Hank behind a yellowish filter, his name in bold white letters and underneath, in smaller yellow letters: 'With Farmer, Silver, Watkins, Blakey'. And, of course, the music does sound like original, vintage early Messengers music, even though Farmer is now in the trumpet chair. His sound, style and general jazz approach were not really in any way different to Kenny Dorham's; only their individual tones differed. Although the music is played to a very high standard throughout, the first thing of note on this disc is the compositions. All were written by Mobley and all are intriguing and stimulating originals; interesting enough as melodic and harmonic structures as well as being ideal vehicles for improvised choruses. Perhaps most striking of all is the ballad 'Fin de l'Affair', a bitter-sweet melody that sounds as though it could have come from the pen of Irving Berlin or Cole Porter or any of the masters of the American popular song. Excellent as the vast majority of Hank's original compositions were, it is the ballad format in which he excelled as a composer. Numerous examples will be found scattered throughout his Blue Note albums from 1955 onwards, beginning with 'My Sin' from *The Hank Mobley Quartet*.

The other highlight of this set is the last piece, 'Base on Balls', a slow, evocative minor blues that begins with Watkins' deep blue bass walking a typical introduction before Silver enters with funky piano and paves the way for the soulful, preaching tenor saxophone of the leader. It is perhaps fitting that the classic Messengers rhythm section should go out on records in much the same way that they came in, playing a slow blues, walked in by Watkins, as they did on 'Room 608' on *Horace Silver and the Jazz Messengers* from 1954.

Sadly, though, the jazz life was about to take its toll on Hank and the addiction that began sometime in 1957 plagued him for most of the rest of his life and probably contributed to his relatively early death. Typically honest and forthright, he told Litweiler in 1973 that he had gone into it with his eyes open and blamed nobody but himself. 'I had the knowledge,' he said:

> When I got strung out it was my own fault. A person getting strung out at eighteen; that's a problem. He doesn't even have a chance to learn what life is about. By the time I got strung out I had learned my instrument. I was making money. Now, I don't have to worry about drugs – I've had enough of that whole thing. All of us are finished with it, it's a thing of the past now.

Interestingly, the last two sentences of Hank's statement indicate that he was off drugs for the last years of his life and virtually all the rest of the bebop musicians who had survived, despite following Parker's disastrous example, were off them too. Today, most musicians – all of the sensible ones – keep well away from hard drugs.

Mobley may have gone into drug addiction with his eyes open but in due course he paid a high price and suffered as much as the majority of addicts. His friend Sonny Rollins went to a clinic and got himself cleaned up, as did Jackie McLean, John Coltrane and a few others later. But Hank continued using throughout the 1950s and 1960s and watched bassist Paul Chambers, pianists Sonny Clark and Bobby Timmons, and bassist Doug Watkins die young as a direct result of the jazz life. Watkins fell asleep at the wheel of his car in Arizona, driving through the night with the aim of joining Philly Joe Jones and Elmo Hope in a new trio in California, but the others, all of whom had worked regularly with Mobley in clubs and on record, were victims of heroin addiction in one way or another. And being an addict meant that you needed a lot of money to survive. Like his friend John Coltrane, Hank worked every hour he could get in New York City, which involved club work, concerts (occasionally) and whatever you could get in the recording studios, as leader or sideman. At that time, the independent labels had a penchant for putting unlikely combinations of saxophonists and trumpeters together in the studio and just letting them get on with it. On two dates with Coltrane, for Prestige in 1956, it had really been a case of just going into the studio and blowing cold.

Prestige had lined up Mobley and Coltrane for *Two Tenors* in May 1956. Hank told writer J. C. Thomas[3] that the record had originally been issued under pianist Elmo Hope's name but later came out as a 'Coltrane–Mobley' disc when he, and particularly Coltrane, started to make names for themselves. Mobley claimed that Prestige lined it up because they wanted to repeat the success of the earlier Gene Ammons–Sonny Stitt two-tenor albums. He also said that he had suggested some of the tunes used. Then came the four-tenor line-up for *Tenor Conclave* on September 7th 1956, and finally Blue Note, not to be outdone, had Johnny Griffin, Coltrane and Mobley all together for *A Blowing Session* on April 6th 1957.

Mobley's comments about this session are illuminating. Talking to John Litweiler as late as 1973, he claimed that if you played with Johnny Griffin or Coltrane, it was hard work. 'You have to out-psych them. They'd say, "Let's play 'Cherokee'." I'd go, "naw, naw – ah, how about a little 'Bye Bye Blackbird'?" I put my heavy form on them, then I can double up and do everything I want to do.' Later he told Litweiler: 'Johnny called a very fast tune, and I said, "Wait a minute." I walked around, they said, "Hank, what's wrong?" I had to get it together, get my tempo together, play my speed.' Obviously not averse to using a little psychology, Mobley doubtless used this method to slow down the pace and buy himself a little time for composure. He must have known he would need to handle fast tempi with those two and he also knew that he was capable of doing so, if necessary. Compare his comments to J. C. Thomas about this session in the early 1970s:

> Griffin is a speed merchant, a really fast tenor player. I remember I got into two false starts on 'The Way You Look Tonight', because Johnny was setting such a fast tempo and still playing cool. Trane didn't have any trouble keeping up with him, and he was making Johnny work like a sprinter hustling for the finish line. Now I pride myself on being able to play fast, too, but whoo-ee, what a workout.

It may have been hard work and a killing tempo that Mobley would not usually have employed but I remain convinced that he was always equal to it, and knew it. On the subject of the two-, three- and four-tenor line-ups of the mid-1950s, John Litweiler remarked:

> What often remains memorable is Mobley's warmth and lyric fluency . . . The sensitivity that his style is based on is perhaps best revealed by his rhythmic flexibility: the sense of contrast is internalised, he becomes a succession of Hank Mobleys as he plays. The style is notable for his love of the middle registers, the odd rhythmic shifts, the perfection of a complex sense of melody (straight-ahead versus decorative playing) that makes the structural evolution viable.[4]

Listening again to 'The Way You Look Tonight', it is true enough that Griffin, and later Coltrane, sound completely at ease at the ultra-fast tempo. But, apart from his bluesy sound and a few characteristic squeals, Griffin plays it pretty straight and is really just running the changes at high velocity. Hank certainly does not sound as comfortable with the tempo as the other two, but there is rather more variety in his improvised choruses than in Griffin's and he is fluent and warm lyrically. 'All the Things You Are' is taken at a more relaxed tempo and Griffin's sound is richer and more robust on this track, although, even here, he often reverts to doubling the tempo. Coltrane is more inventive and at ease also and Hank, sailing out to his solo after Lee Morgan's trumpet interlude, is both melodically interesting and rhythmically complex although, miraculously, he swings along in almost studied, nonchalant fashion. The record as a whole is really just a straight-ahead blowing session, as the title indicates, interesting only for the contrasting styles of the three tenor saxophonists, the relief provided by Morgan's trumpet forays and a fine, swinging rhythm section comprising Wynton Kelly on piano, bassist Paul Chambers and Art Blakey at the drums. This section would make a considerable contribution to Mobley's most productive and fascinating eighteen months in music in the early 1960s. But when he linked up with his fellow tenor players in 1957, that period of ultra-creative energy and accomplishment was still three years away.

5

Poppin' and the Curtain Call Session

Although 1957 was a remarkably active and creative year for Mobley, much of his output went unnoticed at the time because it was eclipsed by the more fashionable (and highly publicised) sounds emanating from the tenor saxophones of Sonny Rollins and John Coltrane. Indeed, Coltrane produced his classic *Blue Train* session for Blue Note towards the end of that year. It was highly praised, and deservedly so. Trane had a high-profile berth in the important Miles Davis Quintet during this time and Miles' group was approaching a peak of performance with the tenor saxist emerging as one of the most gifted and original on his instrument. Rollins, too, had been busy making a name for himself in 1956 with his classic album, *Saxophone Colossus*, and through working with the popular Max Roach–Clifford Brown Quintet. In 1957 he recorded important albums for Riverside and Blue Note as well as Les Koenig's Contemporary label in California.

With these two musicians setting new standards for jazz saxophone, it would be easy to write Hank Mobley off as just another also-ran on the instrument, but Mobley was not in competition with anybody and was not looking nervously over his shoulder at everything Trane and Sonny did. Indeed, he was probably unaware of their activities most of the time. Like any really special, innovative musician, he was getting on with his own music, developing and refining it and playing in public and on records as frequently as he could. He recorded six LPs for Blue Note in 1957 although, inexplicably, *Curtain Call* and *Poppin'*, made towards the end of the year, were not issued in the USA by Blue Note. They were both issued as Japanese Blue Note LPs many years later (*Curtain Call* as *Hank Mobley Quintet Featuring Sonny Clark*) and eventually saw the light of day in western countries more than twenty years after the recording dates, both as Japanese imports and more recently as part of the six-CD limited edition boxed set from Mosaic Records (*The Complete Blue Note Hank Mobley Fifties Sessions*).

On the road, Mobley worked for Horace Silver in the quintet built up from the original Messengers of 1954 but, by spring of 1957, bassist Watkins had gone out as a freelance musician and Teddy Kotick had taken his place with Horace. Then Hank swapped places with tenor saxist Cliff Jordan from the Max Roach group as Silver got Jordan, and Mobley returned to his old boss Roach.

Mobley's playing was getting better and better, both in the recording studio and, according to contemporary reports, on live club dates. He was, after all, consolidating a style which was just as valid as Rollins' if not as influential and far-reaching as Coltrane but, like Lester Young in the 1930s and 1940s, he was oblivious to other people's methods and concerned only with refining his own, special sound. In the 1960s, critic Nat Hentoff would quote Donald Byrd in the sleeve note for the LP *Far Away Lands*: 'Hank is to me just as much a personality as Sonny Rollins. I mean, he has so definitely established his own sound and style.'[1] And that was the opinion of many jazz musicians, but the public did not notice and the jazz press did not applaud what he was doing.

On April 21st 1957 Mobley recorded a supercharged set called simply *Hank* (Blue Note 1560). *Hank* has a sterling cast comprising Donald Byrd, John Jenkins on alto, pianist Bobby Timmons, Wilbur Ware on bass, and the great Philly Joe Jones at the drums. With such a fiery rhythm section, this one was always going to be a real burner but, compared to records by Coltrane or Rollins at the time, sales were modest, perhaps because Mobley continued to refine his warm, round sound and many jazz enthusiasts wrote him off as just another Lester Young-inspired cool cat and looked to Trane and Rollins for the sounds of the future.

But Mobley continued to plough his own furrow, content that he was doing so as well as he possibly could. With his rare gifts of rhythmic ingenuity, and a softer sound than other leading tenor players at that time, his playing nevertheless reflected the hard bop manner of playing and, particularly, phrasing.

If *Curtain Call*, which was recorded on August 18th, had been issued in the late 1950s, it might have commanded very good sales as it reunited Mobley and trumpeter Kenny Dorham, partners in the original Messengers band. It was also the first time (at least in the recording studio) that the splendid, but then underrated, pianist Sonny Clark worked with Mobley. Bassist Jimmy Rowser (wrongly credited as George Joyner on those original Japanese issues) and drummer Art Taylor made up a highly serviceable rhythm section.

The *Curtain Call* set is full of good, vintage Mobley and some fine examples of that charismatic teaming with Dorham. The sound produced by the trumpeter was burnished and warm, something like that of Miles Davis or Art Farmer, but not quite. It was individual and had a trace of the 'hot' trumpet style associated with Gillespie, Fats Navarro and Clifford Brown. Listeners might confuse Art Farmer with Chet Baker occasionally, or Miles Davis even, but there was never any danger that Dorham would sound like anybody but himself. That, perhaps, was one of the reasons he and Mobley welded together so seamlessly in the Messengers and on sessions such as *Curtain Call*.

On 'Don't Get Too Hip', from this set, the relaxed swing from the rhythm section sets up both Dorham and Mobley for solo statements that are, in fact, ultra-hip in spite of the title. A long introductory solo from Sonny Clark sets the mood very efficiently and everybody falls into an easy groove that lasts for the entire eleven minutes of the Mobley composition. The title track 'Curtain Call' is, by complete contrast, an up-tempo swinger in the classic hard bop mould and Hank scorches a path in his opening solo with Jimmy Rowser and Art Taylor spurring him on. Dorham follows and shows how easily he could burn up the bop changes and still sound relaxed and in complete control. Clark, too, is an old hand at fast, almost glib piano lines and his sparkling solo here is a real gem. Clark introduces and sets up the romantic ballad 'Deep in a Dream', much as he did for tenor saxist Ike Quebec four years later on his LP *Leapin' And Lopin'* (Blue Note 84091). Hank responds with a luxurious, soft-focus tenor solo full of pathos.

In 1957, *Curtain Call* was one of Hank's best records to date, close in quality to the all star set with Milt Jackson in January 1957. The prime characteristic of this thoroughly enjoyable session is relaxation. Perhaps because the two 'ultra-hip' (as Horace Silver described them) front-liners were together again and feeling comfortable with each other, the effect is like a swinging supersession where everybody is at his best. Sonny Clark certainly plays a major part in this success story and the lesser-known Jimmy Rowser gives a surprisingly good account of himself together with the ever reliable Art Taylor.

It is worth considering too that if this disc had been released in the USA and consequently heard round the world, it would certainly have confounded those sceptics who claimed that Mobley was an erratic and unreliable soloist in the 1950s. They would have had to acknowledge that by 1957 he was completely the master of his own style and good enough to compete with any other soloist on his instrument as an original stylist. Listen particularly to his solo on 'Deep in a Dream', not the easiest ballad to negotiate and play with ease. Mobley's interpretation is both skilled and highly original with the personal stamp that marks the true improviser.

Mobley recorded an LP two months later, on October 20th, that was in many ways even better. *Poppin'* featured Art Farmer, baritone saxophonist Pepper Adams, and a tough, hard-swinging rhythm section comprising Clark once again but this time with Paul Chambers on bass and Philly Joe Jones at the drums. Listening to all the tracks on this disc, the solos, the original compositions and the fiery, yet highly sympathetic contributions from the rhythm section, I am forced to the conclusion that Alfred Lion just had too much material on the shelf and not enough time or resources to put it all out, even when it was of high quality. With the admitted exception of Coltrane's *Blue Train* and possibly Sonny Rollins' splendid *Newk's Time* sessions, *Poppin'* is as good as anything recorded by the company in 1957 and better than the vast majority of releases that did find their way to the record retailers' shops. Farmer, Adams and Clark are on top form

Questioned many years later about *Poppin'* and many other sets that were never released at the time, Lion always replied that he was surprised certain high-quality sessions had not come out and claimed that the company was so busy at the time that many LPs just got shelved temporarily and then, instead of release at a later time, were forgotten in the rush to keep up with the new material that was being recorded every few days. Held over due to pressure of work and then forgotten is the most reasonable and logical reason for such a fine session as *Poppin'* not hitting the high street shops soon after it was recorded, although severe lack of finance must also, I suppose, be a contender.

It was on the liner notes to this recording, finally released in the 1980s, that Larry Kart made the following highly perceptive observation about Mobley's abilities:

> Equipped with all the skills of a great improviser, Mobley simply refuses to perform the final act of integration; he will not sum up his harmonic, rhythmic, and timbral virtues and allow any one element to dominate for long. In that sense he is literally a pioneer, a man whose innate restlessness never permits him to plant a flag and say, 'Here I stand.'[2]

Kart goes on to say that it would be inappropriate to speak of a mature or immature Hank Mobley and that once certain technical problems were worked out, by about 1955, he was capable of producing striking music on any given day and, on the day of recording *Poppin'*, 'He was as likely as ever to be "on".'

This is a good analysis and goes completely against the often quoted opinion that Hank's early work, between 1954 and 1957, was lacking in inventiveness and structure. The overall impression left on the listener is of a soloist ploughing a lonely furrow but reaping a rich harvest albeit almost by accident at times.

If *Poppin'* represents the high point of Mobley's recordings during 1957, his first Blue Note set of 1958, *Peckin' Time*, recorded on February 9th, sounds almost staid and routine by comparison. It was his first record as a leader where he had the support of Wynton Kelly on piano, a man who was due to play a significant part on a later series of discs in 1960. Paul Chambers was the bassist and although he had featured on previous Mobley-led sessions, his combination with Kelly and with drummer Charli Persip on this album was not as compelling as the later meetings with either Art Blakey or Philly Joe Jones were to prove. All of which is not to deny that *Peckin' Time* is a first-class set. Mobley is just as relaxed as on previous releases and all the compositions, with the exception of 'Speak Low', are his own. He also has the stimulating presence of Lee Morgan in the front line with him, a reminder of his first session on Savoy in 1956. Morgan was a man whose fiery sound and constant inventiveness always kept Hank on his toes and brought out the best in him. But, although 1958 began brightly with the *Peckin' Time* record date and regular work in the clubs, it was the beginning of a very rough period in Mobley's life, fuelled by drugs. It is significant that he recorded ten records as a leader in 1956 and six in 1957, but after *Peckin' Time* there were no more in 1958 and there was a complete blank in 1959.

Apart from a productive and stimulating spell back with Art Blakey and Lee Morgan in the Jazz Messengers and a few other sideman appearances, 1959 was a bad year for the saxophonist. He was on the slide and would need all his powers of invention and originality to pick himself up again.

6

Soul Station

When I first started listening seriously to jazz in the mid to late 1950s, it was not possible to buy Blue Note records in the UK. A good slice of the Prestige output was issued under licence by Esquire Records in this country and you could get a number of Atlantic LPs that were released on London Records. Vogue put out Pacific Jazz and a very few Blue Note sessions, but in the main we were starved of music from a premier jazz catalogue. So it was particularly rewarding in the early 1960s when Blue Note LPs began to be imported into the UK and my first purchases were *The Jazz Messengers*, the 1958 *Moanin'* session with Lee Morgan and Bobby Timmons and V*olume Two* (because only *Volume Two* was available for a long time) of *The Jazz Messengers at the Café Bohemia* with, as fate would have it, Hank Mobley and Kenny Dorham in the front line.

I was immediately knocked out by Mobley's playing on the Bohemia disc, even though it was a relatively early sample, and in spite of the fact that the jazz community have kept pretty quiet about his tenor work here over the years. Even so, there was quite a leap in his abilities as a soloist in the next five years and my second purchase of a Mobley record was *Soul Station*, shortly after it came out in 1960 or early 1961. I could not know at the time that Mobley was just hitting his prime and that the new LP was the first of three which would represent the finest recorded music of his entire career, but I still have the original Blue Note LP. I play it regularly as the sound is better, less bland, than the Van Gelder-remastered CD version. *Soul Station* is Hank Mobley's masterpiece.

* * *

On 7th February 1960, Mobley travelled to Englewood Cliffs, New Jersey, to record at Rudy Van Gelder's new, custom-built studio. There could have been no idea in his head at the time that this was anything other than a routine recording session for Blue Note, one of many he had undertaken for the company since his first as a leader in 1955. The idea that anything special would result from the few hours spent taping the session would not have occurred to any of the musicians present. Among them, drummer Art Blakey, like Philly Joe Jones, was ideal for Mobley, with his unique ideas about rhythm. These two men could follow Hank anywhere and enhance his lines no matter how quirky they might sound to the world at large. The pianist for the session, Wynton Kelly, was known as one of the very best accompanists in the business. The fourth member of the group was Paul Chambers, the young master-bassist of the era. The session was a quartet date, with Hank as the only horn, as on his very first disc as a leader (*The Hank Mobley Quartet*) back in 1955.

The musicians recorded three originals by the leader, one blues and two unhackneyed, but very attractive standards. The end result was *Soul Station*, one of the greatest LPs to emerge from Blue Note Records in the 1950s and 1960s. It was cited by British tenor saxophonist and club owner Ronnie Scott as his favourite Mobley album and it is, and has remained, the acknowledged best of all Hank's records for many musicians and enthusiasts ever since it was released in 1960.

Listening constantly to the music on this LP, and later on the CD reissue and analysing it, does not really give any clue to the sudden maturity of style and conception that is evident, but there may well be a physical reason to explain the strength and warmth of Mobley's tenor saxophone sound. Writing in the March 2004 edition of *Jazz Journal International*, Simon Spillett, an impressive young jazz tenor saxophonist himself and a staunch admirer of Mobley, states:

> there is a greater depth and clarity to his tone, possibly attributed to his finally settling upon a metal Otto Link mouthpiece. which gives a far broader open quality when compared to the fogginess of Hank's work on his previous ebonite mouthpiece during the mid-1950s

The new mouthpiece would certainly have made a difference to the overall sound and a second point made by Spillett is also a major factor in the success of the disc: Mobley's choice of sidemen.

In 1978, four British jazz critics named *Soul Station* as one of the two hundred modern jazz records that no enthusiast should be without.[1] Reviewing the LP, Michael James wrote:

> This LP set the seal on Mobley's complete emergence as an inventive and personal improviser, and though some of his subsequent releases bear comparison with it, none presents a more favourable impression of his accomplishments.

The review suggests that, prior to this recording, Mobley was a gifted stylist but his phrasing, relying on his idiosyncratic use of rhythm, often suffered if his sense of timing or accuracy of note production went slightly askew. It also suggests that it had seemed that up until this point Mobley might never achieve his promise. However I rather think that he was well on his way with sessions such as the 1955 LP *The Hank*

Mobley Quartet*, the 1957 LP *Hank Mobley and His All Stars* and the unreleased *Poppin'*.

Certain special records strike a chord with musicians, reviewers, historians and fans, and it is frequently the case that the greatest individual soloists have one outstanding disc that outstrips all their other efforts in terms of invention, inspiration and quality of music. With Louis Armstrong it happened early on, with his Hot Fives and Hot Sevens from 1925 to 1927. Parker, too, peaked relatively early, and his Savoy sessions from 1945, particularly the tracks on the later-released LP such as 'Ko Ko', 'Billie's Bounce' and 'Thriving on a Riff', represent classic Bird in full flight, rampant with invention. Parker and Gillespie had *The Quintet – Jazz at Massey Hall* from 1952 and Miles Davis had *Kind of Blue* in 1959. Sonny Rollins had taped *Saxophone Colossus* in 1956 and John Coltrane made his *A Love Supreme* in 1967. With Hank Mobley it was February 1960 and *Soul Station* is his undisputed masterpiece.

Considering the success of *The Hank Mobley Quartet* in 1955, it is surprising that he left it so long before attempting to make another LP with only his own horn in the front line and a world-class rhythm section. It seems, with the benefit of that useful measuring tool, hindsight, that he could have produced more successful records with a quartet and no second or third horn partners. And a case could be made, although not a very strong one, for suggesting that Hank's two quartet discs from 1955 and 1960 represent his finest work on records.

Arguably *Soul Station* is, in all respects, just about the perfect jazz album. From the relaxed, opening bars of Irving Berlin's 'Remember' through to the last notes of the ballad 'If I Should Lose You', Hank and his sterling rhythm section are on inspired form. And when talking about the one recorded set that great soloists all seem to produce, a CD that stands out from the rest as special, it is surprising how many of these discs are made by a quartet. *Saxophone Colossus*, Coltrane's *A Love Supreme* and *Giant Steps*, his Atlantic LP from 1959 which would also qualify as a masterwork, spring readily to mind, along with *Soul Station* and, of course, Mobley's first strong quartet date for Blue Note. A little later in that crucial year, 1960, Hank recorded *Roll Call*, another masterpiece which some commentators have claimed is almost the equal of *Soul Station*. It isn't. *Soul Station* stands alone; perhaps we should take a close look at it to find out if and why my statement is valid.

Joe Goldberg's perceptive and very well-informed liner notes give us our first clues and it is worth remembering that when he wrote them, and indeed when the record was first released in the late spring of 1960, Mobley was still receiving lukewarm recognition or downright negative criticism from critics for his work, both live and on recordings. Goldberg begins by dismissing the notion that LPs such as this should be regarded as just a 'blowing date'.[2] He argues that only the very greatest jazz musicians could get away with just coming into the studio and blowing, with little or no preparation. And while the record seems on the surface to have all the elements of a 'blowing session': 'tenor and rhythm, a few originals, a couple of seldom-done standards, and a blues', the difference, according to Goldberg, is apparent as soon as you start listening. He goes on to suggest that two of the factors that make the LP outstanding and different from run-of-the-mill products of the time are the presence of Art Blakey on drums and Hank's unusual rhythm sense. He quotes from a conversation with Blakey where the drummer noted that many songs are written in complex rhythms but the soloists almost always revert to a straight 4/4 time. Blakey maintained that most of them couldn't play them any other way but that Hank Mobley could. It is no accident that all analysis of Mobley's solo abilities refer to his unique and very personal rhythmic prowess. His methods may have been quirky, eccentric even, at times, but his ability to swing and fit all his phrases into the required time structure are essential to his success and belated recognition as a truly different, and original, jazz soloist.

Taking up Goldberg's point about Blakey for a moment: he was the drummer on Hank's first Blue Note disc and with the cooperative group of Jazz Messengers where Mobley first matured as a soloist and he would also feature on Mobley's later album, *Roll Call*. Certainly Art opens up this set from bar one and is an inspiration throughout the session. 'Remember' is a seldom tackled, attractive Irving Berlin song and Mobley and everybody else sound completely relaxed throughout this reading. Hank sails inventively through his solos flanked by the impeccable rhythmic thrust and support provided by Kelly, Chambers and Blakey. Next up, Mobley's own 'This I Dig of You', is a compulsive swinger where the leader, Kelly and Blakey, in particular, distinguish themselves. Blakey's solo is stunning; all of his kit is utilised in a polyrhythmic *tour de force* that sounds like no other drum solo I have ever heard. No wonder the leader and the other sidemen were inspired to play at the top of their abilities. It is often forgotten, or barely understood, that for all the jokes about three musicians and a drummer, a top percussionist, in inspired form, can lift the performances of all the musicians on the date and cap them with an abundance of energy and a special lift from his own contributions. Art Blakey does that here and is certainly a major factor in the success of this album.

Wynton Kelly's special brand of light touch, melodic soloing ability and intuitive, sympathetic accompaniment, is another strong factor and he, too, was on top form for this recording date. He and Chambers had played together on records and in the Miles Davis Quintet and Sextet rhythm section for some years and they worked hand in glove together at all times. With

Blakey they were a pretty lethal combination and when they were 'hot', as here, any soloist would find it more difficult not to swing than to swing easily. Add to that the fact that there was no other horn soloist to add another dimension of only partial compatibility or his own agenda. All these factors played their part in producing an exceptional LP in an era when exceptional LPs were far more frequent than they are today. We have, however, left the most important consideration to last: Mobley himself.

Goldberg, in those original LP notes, talks about the difficulty in categorising the tenor man. Mobley always presented problems for jazz writers because, unlike almost every other contemporary musician, he could not easily be fitted into slots beloved of such writers, as, for example, an out and out bopper, hard bopper, cool player, or even as someone influenced, directly or indirectly, by the major players of the day: Sonny Rollins, John Coltrane or early pacesetters like Coleman Hawkins and Lester Young. Hank stood alone, as always. And as Goldberg pointed out, his strongest influence had been Charlie Parker, not Lester Young as many people believe. His sound was not lightweight or cool like Lester and his stylistic descendants. What had happened to Hank, to bring him to the creative peak he reached with *Soul Station*, was, according to Goldberg, 'so simple as to be completely overlooked, in a mass of theory, digging for influences, and the like: he was working out his own style'. As Goldberg saw it,

> he worked slowly and carefully, in the manner of a craftsman . . . taking what he needed to take from whomever he needed to take it (everyone does that, the difference between genius and hackwork is the manner in which it is done) and finally emerging, on this album, not with a disconnected series of tunes, but with a definite statement to make.

It sounds like an oversimplification, but you won't find me giving Joe Goldberg an argument. The level of relaxation that Hank displays on the title track is far greater than anything evident on his records up to that point and the creative process thus seems to become effortless. His lines flow with such ease and fluidity that he commands a special effort from his rhythm section and they respond spontaneously.

All the above is fairly obvious now, more than forty years after the event, but it is a safe bet that none of it would have been apparent at the time. The musicians would probably have been pleased that the session went particularly well and left it at that. Reaction to the LP was good but hardly ecstatic. The reviewer in the American magazine *DownBeat* gave it four stars, which means 'very good', along with a warm but far from rapturous review. Today, if it were appearing for the first time, it would almost certainly receive the five-star 'excellent' rating and a string of written superlatives.

Talking about the three most productive years of Mobley's life in *Jazz Journal* (September 1986), Dave Gelly made the following observations about 'This I Dig of You' from *Soul Station*:

> It was during these few glorious years that he demonstrated most effectively his ability to improvise on both modal and chromatic harmonies and to move between the two with absolute stylistic consistency. Listen to 'This I Dig of You' on *Soul Station*, which alternates eight bars of one scale (Cm7/F7) with eight bars of chromatic changes. The first winds up the spring and the second releases it. The sheer agility with which he exploits this musical drama is enough to place him in the ranks of the great jazz improvisers. Listen too to his brisk, spare statement of the theme of 'Remember', the clear, measured lines in the stop time choruses of the blues 'Dig Dis' and the calm, knowing exploration of 'If I Should Lose You'. *Soul Station* is Hank Mobley's masterpiece, on a par with Rollins' *Saxophone Colossus*.

The cover of the original LP and all subsequent CD issues shows a black-and-white photograph, taken with a blue filter, of Hank smiling broadly and holding up his saxophone in a sort of salute of triumph. Perhaps, as that photograph was taken, he did have a suspicion that the recording he had just completed was something special and his career was entering a new, more mature, phase.

7

Working Out

After the taping of *Soul Station* in February 1960, Mobley began a sustained period of work both in clubs and on records where he was at the absolute height of his powers. The late 1950s had been a period of turmoil and trouble with drug problems forcing him out of active work and recording and even a brief prison sentence.

He had returned to the Jazz Messengers for a time in 1959 and can be heard playing, and playing very well, along with old friends such as Lee Morgan and Bobby Timmons on a two-LP set for Blue Note called *The Jazz Messengers at the Jazz Corner of the World*. This was one of Blakey's many returns to Birdland but because of a link-up with another record company at the time, Blue Note were not allowed to name the location, hence 'The Jazz Corner of the World', although everybody knew that was another name for Birdland. Despite being recorded live and having some sterling hard boppers in the ranks, these two albums present some easy-going music with even Lee Morgan a little more subdued than usual and Hank as relaxed as he ever appeared on record. Mobley contributed three compositions to the programme, including two which appeared on *Volume One*: 'Hipsippy Blues', a loping twelve-bar, and 'Just Coolin'', the latter harking back to his first quartet recording for Blue Note. 'Hipsippy' ambles along gently at a leisurely pace but features intriguing solos by both Morgan and Mobley.

The next track on *Volume One* is a Thelonious Monk piece, 'Justice'. Mobley had spent a short time playing in Monk's quartet but had not recorded with the pianist and his stay has tended to be rather obscure and underexposed. At a fairly fast tempo, Hank's solo is a snaking, individualistic swinger but I can't say that it sounds much like a Monk composition and it could be that Mobley was too much of a unique and personal soloist to fit in with Monk's requirements for a sideman. That may be why his time in the quartet was so brief. Generally on these live sides, Mobley is in typically warm and inventive form and Blakey must have been glad to have him back in the ranks, albeit for a relatively short while.

So, putting the disappointments and hard times of 1958–59 firmly behind him, Mobley had made his most successful record in February 1960 and returned to Englewood Cliffs on November 13th of the same year to record *Roll Call* for Blue Note. He wisely chose to bring back Wynton Kelly and Paul Chambers, along with the explosive Art Blakey. And for contrast with his relatively mellow tenor, he added the fiery trumpet of Freddie Hubbard, a young musician just beginning to make a name for himself in 1960. But if the personnel was identical to that of his last LP, with the addition of a well-regarded trumpet player, the music was not the same, far from it. Where *Soul Station* represented the soul of relaxed bop, *Roll Call* is, by complete contrast, a fiery, at times burning, session. Part of the reason for this may be Hubbard; he had recently emerged as a player in the tradition of Dizzy Gillespie and, even more so, Clifford Brown and Fats Navarro. Hubbard's tone was bright and brassy and he played with enormous composure and a very big sound for someone so young. With such a player in the ranks (and it is worth bearing in mind that sidemen were chosen as often by Alfred Lion as by the young leaders in those days) Hank may have felt the edge of competition and decided to play in a fairly strong, hard bop style.

As indicated earlier, Hubbard's comments on the sleeve notes to *Roll Call* are very revealing. At one point he said to annotator Robert Levin that Mobley was his favourite tenor player and: 'He sure plays relaxed.' Mostly Mobley did, although this is one of the rare sessions where he cuts loose and burns up chord changes rapidly and at fairly high volume on more than one track. Bearing in mind that Hubbard was only in his early twenties at the time – his comments about his enjoyment of the date offer further enlightenment:

> I think it was my best date so far. Everything had a nice feeling. I was glad to be there – I learned a lot about how to swing, just being there. I felt so much freer than I had ever before in a recording studio and that's because it's so easy to play with the kind of talent of the guys on the date. And we had just about the best rhythm section there is – Blakey, um, oh, yes! He fills up the whole studio, he makes you open up – he made everyone open up.

So the same soloist with the same rhythm section and one really bright, precocious young trumpeter produced a hard bop session that was far more aggressive and thrusting than the earlier date. The quality of the music, however, was consistent. If *Roll Call* falls short of the standard set by *Soul Station* it is not by very much. The album was another success and has been growing in reputation for more than forty years now. The fact that there was a considerable difference in the style of the music and the general approach of the leader only went to show how versatile he was. Even so, one or two critics, including the *DownBeat* reviewer, chose to praise Hubbard as a bright young hope for the future at the expense of Mobley, whose contribution was described as 'unexceptional'.

This was a good year for Hank in terms of personal appearances and two of his best ever LPs. But, although he must have known they were good, critical reaction was still sparing and even the best notices were hardly over-enthusiastic. It would be many long years before those two records would be recognised as the classics they surely are but, in the meantime, Hank needed to earn a living.

In January 1961 he was hired by Miles Davis to replace John Coltrane in his quintet. At that time Miles had the best known and highest paid combo in jazz and Hank must have felt a sense of security being the tenor sax soloist in such a high-profile band. Unfortunately, most of the sidemen in Davis' quintet were heavily into hard drugs and although the leader himself had been clean for several years, he was faced with the problem of at least two of his musicians constantly getting 'high' or drunk or, in the case of bassist Paul Chambers, both. The man most heavily and dangerously into hard drugs was drummer Philly Joe Jones. Although he had left (or been sacked by) Miles around 1958 and most people tend to think that his tenure with Miles ended at that point, he frequently appeared on the bandstand as a replacement for Jimmy Cobb, when the latter was unavailable or had other gigs.

Mobley claimed that when he left Miles, he was so tired of music and the world in general that he drifted back to drugs. It is difficult, however, to understand how Mobley would have remained immune to all the ferocious drug taking going on around him in the Davis band.

When he was interviewed by Litweiler in 1973, Mobley talked about a trip to Los Angeles with Davis and arriving in that city about five minutes before the plane took off, presumably for the return journey. Hank says he was with Philly Joe

Jones and this must have been sometime between 1961 and 1963. Mobley spoke of the difficulty of getting anywhere in Los Angeles, with no walkways: 'You can't get anywhere. You take Wynton Kelly, he's probably over at that hotel partying and talking about, "yeah, see you when I get back" – him and Paul Chambers. Miles is off talking to Boris Karloff – he and Miles lived in the same house on the strip in Hollywood.'

Later in the same article Mobley talks about having to get Harold Lovette (Miles' lawyer) to take care of business, tidy up the tax – after six nights: 'Wynton had about a $50 [drinks] tab. Paul must've had about fifty. Miles must've had a couple hundred. We hung out, the four of us and sometimes we'd run into Miles in the street.'

It doesn't take much imagination to picture Hank, Wynton Kelly, Paul Chambers and Philly Joe Jones, on the loose in Los Angeles, running up additional drink tabs – this was 1961 or 1962, when $50 was a lot of spending money (more than the average male weekly wage in the UK) – and having a pretty wild time. And if the other three were high on drink and heroin most of the time, what was Mobley doing? Well, whatever he was or wasn't doing in his private life, his professional life was going well. After 1960, 1961 was even better with dates as a leader for Blue Note, and several recordings for the same company as a sideman for Kenny Drew, Freddie Hubbard and others, including the job of providing much of the melodic content on a session co-led by two of the premier modern drummers of the day: Elvin Jones and Philly Joe Jones on their Atlantic LP *Together*.

Hank recorded his next major album as leader, *Workout*, on March 26th 1961 and then, on December 5th, made most of *Another Workout* with the same personnel. The latter was never put out in Alfred Lion's time at Blue Note but eventually surfaced, on LP and later CD, when the company was reactivated in the 1980s. It was long overdue and I wonder in passing if there are yet more undiscovered, unissued Mobley tapes languishing in the Blue Note vaults. At least five CDs were issued just before or soon after Mobley's death in 1986 and all are first-rate recordings.

Hank was certainly aware that many of his recordings were being put to one side and he frequently complained that some of his best work was being held back. As late as 1973 he was still complaining bitterly about Blue Note not issuing his music. 'I wrote a whole movie in Paris,' he told Litweiler:

> It was about the French–Algerian war, and I wrote Algerian and French music, back and forth. Then I came back and recorded it for Blue Note, and they didn't put it out. I had some of the same people I was playing with in New York: Cedar [Walton], Billy [Higgins], Bob Cranshaw, Curtis Fuller, Freddie Hubbard.

He went on to complain that his best record, in his opinion at that time, a brass ensemble disc featuring tenor sax with two trumpets, French horn, alto sax, two trombones, baritone horn and tuba, was unissued and Blue Note refused to release it. Why remains a mystery, but it certainly sounds like an intriguing disc and very different from the run-of-the-mill hard bop product of the time. Perhaps that was the problem. But in 1965 Alfred Lion had sold Blue Note to Liberty Records and in the 1970s Liberty's policy was to change the label over to soul music, funk and fusion so if Mobley's record was hard-core modern jazz, it is no real surprise that they refused to put it out.

Workout, however, is a real hard-swinging burner of a record. Superior in content even to *Roll Call* and second, by a very small margin, to *Soul Station*, it featured the tried and trusted duo of Wynton Kelly on piano and Paul Chambers on bass, plus the bassist's running mate in the 1955–58 Miles Davis band, drummer Philly Joe Jones. These three, who had spent considerable time working together in the Davis band, on records and in live club situations, formed a superb and hard-driving rhythm section. Also featured in the record is guitarist Grant Green.

The title track, 'Workout', roars along with the sort of power and ambience that you get very rarely, but memorably, in a jazz club on a very good night when everything is going exceptionally well and all the musicians are inspired, although this is very rarely translated on to discs, particularly studio recordings. This time it is, and Mobley's charging, emotive solo burns through several inventive choruses before Green and Kelly take blistering solos of their own and Philly Joe wraps up the solo strength with one of his trademark workouts, utilising, as sleeve annotator Leonard Feather pointed out, 'every part of his kit'.

Hank's front-line partner on this disc, Grant Green, was at the time a Blue Note regular in the recording studios and, along with Wes Montgomery, one of the leading bop players on his instrument. After the full brass tone and competitive edge of Freddie Hubbard's trumpet, Green makes a far more relaxed and more appropriate running mate for the saxophonist. The programme is the sort that Hank thrived on, mainly blues, fast or medium tempo, and one good standard, in this case 'The Best Things in Life Are Free', which is given a warm, lyrical reading. 'Uh Huh', the second track, a fascinating Mobley original based on B flat, D flat and E flat, slows the tempo down but keeps up the intensity. Mobley is almost harsh in his opening solo, not like his usual, urbane self, and he squeaks at one point, a mistake which it was most likely felt should be ignored because the solo generally was so expressive and inventive. Of his other originals, 'Smokin'' is up tempo and 'Greasin' Easy' is a medium blues, and in all selections Mobley turns in some of his very best work. Surely he is inspired again, as he was on *Soul*

Station and together these two sets represent the very highest points of his achievement on records.

Mobley recorded 'Three Coins in the Fountain' at the March 26th 1961 session but this track did not find its way on to *Workout* originally. It was added to a much later CD release with this title but first came out in the 1980s on *Another Workout*, an album mostly recorded in December 1961. In the case of these 1961 sessions, Mobley appears to have exactly reversed the procedure of *Soul Station* and *Roll Call*, where a laid-back, relaxed session was followed by a relatively explosive one. This time, the roaring, blues-based *Workout* in March was followed in December by the anodyne *Another Workout*, which had the same personnel minus Grant Green (although his name appeared on early editions of the LP) and tracks like 'I Should Care' and 'Hello Young Lovers' on which Hank sounds, once more, calm and relaxed. An original, 'Hank's Other Soul', is a funky, down-home-type blues of the sort that was becoming almost obligatory at Blue Note in the 1960s and would definitely become so after the success of Lee Morgan's *The Sidewinder* album in 1964.

The reason Hank may have felt so comfortable and completely in control at the *Soul Station* and *Another Workout* sessions could well be that both were quartet dates where he was not in competition with another front-line soloist. Aided by the best rhythm sections to be had in those days, the very private and often reticent man that was Hank Mobley seems to have thrived in the quartet mode. If producers at the time had been more alert to the fact maybe we would have had fewer quintets and sextets and more four-man sessions.

Another Workout represents another departure by Mobley in that three of the six selections are standards and three are Mobley originals. He was a gifted ballad composer and a fine interpreter of other people's efforts, particularly the classic standard American songs of the day. He more than once expressed a desire to record an entire album of slow ballads, but never got round to achieving this goal. Just how good such a disc would have been we can begin to judge by listening to his warm and expressive improvised choruses on 'Hello Young Lovers' and 'I Should Care'. The former is an average type of popular song and the latter a classic ballad. It is a further tribute to Mobley's artistry as an improvising jazzman that, listening to these two readings, it is almost impossible to tell the difference in the original quality of the compositions.

By 1961, Hank's activities were less confined to playing and recording as a leader, which he had begun to do more from 1958 onwards, and more focused on being fully involved as the tenor saxophonist with the Miles Davis Quintet. Davis, reluctant to lose John Coltrane but eventually accepting his departure to become a leader as inevitable, cast around desperately for a suitable replacement to fill those very big shoes. It was an impossible task, of course, and early recruits were none too successful. Jimmy Heath had been first in line but a suspended drug conviction meant he could not travel outside New York City and that was no use to Miles. Next came Sam Rivers, a progressive tenor saxophonist with strong roots in the tradition but perhaps a trifle too 'outside' for Davis at that time. Sonny Stitt worked with the quintet for a while, but by December 8th 1960, when the group played at the Howard Theatre in Washington, Hank Mobley was the new tenor player and when he came in he seemed, on the face of things, to be ideal.

He could play in the hard bop style, albeit with a rather softer sound, he was a great ballad player and he knew all the popular standards that made up eighty per cent of Miles' repertoire at that time. Perhaps most important of all, he could play long, extended solos without repeating himself when Miles abruptly left the bandstand, as he often did, and did not return for an hour or more. And yet Miles was not entirely happy with his new tenor man and often expressed his dissatisfaction in public. In the liner notes to *Someday My Prince Will Come*, trumpeter Eddie Henderson recalls that although Hank was cool and hip:

> Miles would sometimes get mad at Hank, who generally took a while to get his sound together. Hank was from a more traditional school of phrasing, and his swing feel was rooted in this sound (i.e. the Jazz Messengers and Horace Silver). Hank would squeak or fluff, and Miles would pantomime (at the bar) an act of hitting Hank over the head with his trumpet.[1]

When I spoke to tenor saxist/writer Dave Gelly, he suggested that Miles and Hank were alike in many ways, in that both would expect other musicians to fit in with their ways of doing things and this caused friction between the two. Henderson, goes on, however, to suggest that Mobley fitted in very well and was part of the rhythm section's social circle. Certainly Kelly and Chambers had been on Hank's last two Blue Note recordings and would soon appear on a fourth and fifth with the *Workout* sets. He also spent much leisure time at this period in the company of the pianist and bassist, along with drummer Philly Joe Jones. Club appearances during the years from 1959 to 1964 tended to find him with a combination of any of the above musicians as well as Donald Byrd, Elvin Jones, Lee Morgan and Cedar Walton. It is further suggested by Eddie Henderson that this was probably Miles' most popular group in terms of the reaction of black inner-city audiences, mainly due to the availability of recent recordings and the fact that the material was well-known.

At this time Miles played a constant programme of standards such as 'If I Were a Bell', 'On Green Dolphin Street', and 'Stella by Starlight'. This was, in fact, one of the reasons that Coltrane was so anxious to make the break away from Davis: he was weary of playing the same old standards over and over again and anxious to express himself with his own burgeoning pile of original compositions. According to Henderson, who knew Miles well at the time and frequently put him up at his home when the trumpeter played at the Black Hawk in San Francisco, the combination of Mobley, Wynton Kelly, Paul Chambers and Jimmy Cobb related ideally to the black nightclub audience and far better than even the previous sextet that had featured John Coltrane, Cannonball Adderley, Red Garland (or Kelly or Bill Evans depending on who was currently on good terms with Miles), Chambers (a stalwart throughout 1955–62), and Philly Joe Jones or Cobb. That band had played fewer of the old war horses and more 'progressive' bop and blues.

Henderson also argues that by the time Davis disbanded and hired Herbie Hancock, Ron Carter, Tony Williams and Wayne Shorter, the rapport with the black audience had virtually evaporated and he had fewer gigs in the clubs. Maybe this factor helped to steer Davis away from contemporary jazz and into funk and fusion, but that's another story. In any event John Szwed, in his book: *So What: The Life of Miles Davis*, comes to the same conclusion as Henderson. Szwed noted that although Mobley stayed only a year with Miles:

> There was a hipness to his playing that reinforced Davis' popularity in black communities across America . . . There was no shock value with Mobley as with Coltrane's angularity and hyper speed excursions, no kind of floating modal experiments. This band played for the rhythm, re-established its blues credentials, and was not ashamed to swear allegiance to hard bop, that catch-all term that if nothing else signalled blackness.[2]

Ultra-hip or not, Mobley did not manage to please Miles, who was looking for something completely different. In fact they both lost out. Davis, who expected his tenor men to come up with new and highly innovative ways of playing (like

Coltrane and later Wayne Shorter) had to put up with Hank, who may have been hip in the black communities but nevertheless played his own personal brand of contemporary jazz and stayed in his own groove. At the same time, although Mobley was strongly influenced by Miles' approach to music, he did not find the mass acclaim he may well have hoped for through working with Davis. He was seen generally as the villain of the piece for merely being in the band when it was going through a rare period of inertia. But the inertia was really down to Miles Davis; even *he* couldn't keep the music fresh and innovative all the time. In his autobiography he certainly blamed Hank for his own failure to come up with any new music. He said to Quincy Troupe : 'The music was starting to bore me because I didn't like what Hank Mobley was playing in the band. Playing with Hank just wasn't fun for me; he didn't stimulate my imagination.'[3]

So while Hank was producing some of his best solos on records such as *Someday My Prince Will Come* and the *Friday and Saturday Nights at the Blackhawk*, as can be heard particularly on the newly restored solos now that the 'complete' sessions have been made available at last, Miles was seething and waiting for him to become what he was not and could never be, another Coltrane or Shorter. Actually, if that was what he had wanted, the opportunity had presented itself, before Mobley came on board, when Shorter, at the suggestion of John Coltrane, had telephoned Davis to offer his services. And what happened? 'When I want a saxophonist,' Davis had replied, 'I'll let you know,' just before he slammed down the phone.

Miles could sometimes be so cantankerous and difficult that he harmed nobody as much as himself in the process. At any rate, in 1961 he was stuck with Mobley and as Simon Spillett put it in a *Jazz Journal* article:

If anything, Mobley was actually pushing the music backwards. With Davis' huge expectations on his shoulders, one would suspect that Mobley would have felt at best inappropriate, or at worst, inadequate. His response was to do what he did best, that is consolidate rather than innovate.[4]

The problem, as Spillett points out, was Davis' failure to get to grips with his own music at that particular time. After the heady success of the *Kind of Blue* sessions and the three main collaborations with Gil Evans, there was bound to be a dip in form. And that is not to suggest that his output during 1961–62 was in any way poor. By most people's standards, even sub-standard Miles Davis was superior to most of the music being recorded and played during those years. In the long-term view, with the perspective granted by hindsight, however, it can be seen that Davis' dissatisfaction and failure to support his sideman in public was yet another indication that Mobley was seen generally, and would continue to be seen, as a run-of-the-mill saxophonist.

The observations by Henderson and Szwed may also partially explain why Mobley sold a considerable number of LPs and was constantly recorded by Blue Note over a period of fifteen years but never became a really big name in jazz, unlike, for example, Lester Young, Rollins or Coltrane. Like a few other especially talented musicians he had a sort of 'insider' appeal to the black jazz fans, but one that never really spilled over to any great extent to the (considerably bigger overall) white jazz audience. This is only part of the possible explanation for a very strange conundrum, but the very hipness of Mobley, allied to his credentials as a member of the highly successful original Jazz Messengers and his affiliation with both Blakey and Horace Silver's later quintets, may provide part of the answer.

The Miles Davis album *Someday My Prince Will Come* was made over three days in March 1961, when Mobley was already the regular tenor player in the Davis quintet. It is especially interesting because Coltrane also took part in the recording even though he had left Davis and been leading his own highly successful quartet for over a year. This was positively the last occasion when Mobley and Coltrane played together on records and this time, particularly on the title track, Trane eclipsed him with one of his best solos on record from this period. Mobley plays well throughout, but by this time Coltrane had moved up several gears from the always available session man that he had been in 1956 and 1957.

The LP is one of Davis' best and most accessible albums, an amalgam of good, inventive jazz and commercial appeal. If he gave the two tenor saxists their heads on 'Teo' and the title track, the sumptuous ballads 'Old Folks' and 'I Thought About You' are vehicles for his tightly Harmon-muted trumpet and some of his most intense, lyrical improvising. Even so, Mobley shows how well he fitted into this edition of the quintet with a solo that almost matches the leader's on 'Old Folks'. Hank does it again on 'I Thought About You', almost managing to eclipse the leader's strong solo and adapting so easily into the 'quality but commercial' aspect of that Davis band. Had Miles not been so easily bored and so intent on moving ever onwards and searching for new ideas and sounds, even when he couldn't find any, this particular quintet could have lasted several years and kept him popular with a wide-ranging audience base, including the black nightclub set that he often courted but mostly failed to hold on to.

Recorded during this session but not released on the original LP, was 'Blues No. 2', when Philly Joe Jones sat in on drums with Davis' group for the very last time on records although, of course, his association with the trumpeter was continuous until the formation of the radically new quintet with Shorter, Carter and Williams. By that time Philly was bound for England and

France, staying on the Continent to live and play for the next five or so years.

A month later the Davis quintet headed out to San Francisco and the Black Hawk, a dingy, dirty, thoroughly disgusting nightclub which was redeemed by good acoustics and the regular supportive audiences that always included musicians and plenty of hard-core jazz enthusiasts. Recorded over two nights, April 21st and 22nd, the originally released two LPs gave only a sampling of what was, surprisingly, Davis' first live, on-location, recording session. Now we have two double-CD sets that document everything played on those nights and restore many truncated solos from earlier LP and CD issues, many of them Hank Mobley efforts. Again, this is significant because Miles was back to his old habit of economy in all things: play as few notes as possible to make a meaningful musical statement, and stay as little time as possible onstage when you can get off, go and stand at the bar with a drink, and leave the long solos in the capable hands of your saxophonist and pianist. Only if he had complete faith in the ability and staying power of his tenor player would Miles do that, as he had before with John Coltrane.

The two double CDs issued by Sony/Columbia in 2003 offer four hours of live music from the Black Hawk at a time when Miles and his sidemen were at their absolute peak.[5] Around this time, Mobley himself made three of his finest ever albums as leader and his solos on Davis' Black Hawk recordings, restored to their full length here, are up to the same high standards of inventiveness. The new issues also offer the music in chronological order, as it was recorded on the nights, whereas the earlier LPs and CDs had bits from Saturday's sets patched into Friday and vice versa. With the fully restored solos, particularly Hank's as he was the main victim of the excisions, we can hear the full structure through beginning, middle and end, and often marvel at the logic of his overall schemes. These records are important documents in the history of hard bop and as good examples as can be found anywhere of the solo strengths of Miles, Mobley and Kelly. They are very different from Mobley's Blue Notes of the same period but that is because these discs are Miles Davis' records and his personality and methods of presentation are paramount. Miles' later group with Shorter, Hancock and Carter may have been more sophisticated, more advanced in terms of contemporary jazz and more innovative overall, but as far as reaching the people was concerned, as Szwed and Henderson observed, the Black Hawk band was far more direct in its straight-ahead presentation of hard bop and blues.

For Hank Mobley the pace of activity was intensifying throughout 1961. After joining Miles at the very tail-end of 1960, he recorded with him in the studio in January and again in March, then April at the Black Hawk and on May 21st at Carnegie Hall, on a live concert that very nearly missed being taped. In addition there was a round of live dates with Miles that did not get recorded and in March he recorded the two Blue Note sets *Workout* and *Another Workout*. As if all this were not enough to keep him busy, he was in constant demand as a sideman, particularly for Blue Note, and appeared on record sessions for Freddie Hubbard, pianist Kenny Drew, his old running mate with the Messengers Kenny Dorham, and many others. The demand for his music was at an all-time high and the only surprise is that he was not better known and more critically acclaimed at this time.

8

The Turnaround

All the musicians who worked in Miles Davis' various groups learned a lot about their profession from the experience. Even those who were well established before they worked or recorded with the trumpeter have acknowledged the fact. Seasoned musicians such as Lee Konitz and J. J. Johnson, both well established before Davis had begun to make a name for himself, are no exceptions. For Sonny Rollins and John Coltrane, the association was the beginning of their rise as major soloists. Certainly Mobley picked up a lot while working with Miles, as he himself acknowledged:

> Miles pulled my coat to a few things. He suggested just straight ahead, hit every note straight on the head – it's hard to explain. It means, you can play two or three ways; you can play romantic type, the big sound, like that, you can play mathematical, like my man Lee Konitz used to do with Warne Marsh; and the other is similar to Trane, where you hit everything sharp. Every time you try to get an idea across, you don't labour, play behind the beat, or anything like that: you hit it, and bring something out of it.[1]

It is no great surprise that Mobley matured as a major soloist during late 1960 and throughout 1961, given that he was working regularly with just about the most important and innovative combo in jazz. Every soloist who went through those hallowed ranks went on to success of one kind or another in contemporary jazz.

But one double CD, recorded at a prestigious concert at New York's Carnegie Hall by Miles' 1961 quintet with a large orchestra, very nearly went unrecorded. If, like me at the time, you have ever wondered why a big record company like Columbia (now owned by Sony) should make a record with only average quality sound, in mono, as late as 1961, the reason was Miles Davis himself and his quirky ways. As late as the morning of the recording, with trucks full of state-of-the-art recording equipment ready to roll towards the concert hall, Davis telephoned producer Teo Macero and told him he had decided not to let them record the music because most of the selections had been recorded on previous LPs within the past year or so. This was true and only served to reinforce John Coltrane's criticism of Davis, that he played the same old popular songs over and over again.

The concert on May 19th was intended to present performances by the quintet alone, together with others using a twenty-one-piece orchestra directed by Gil Evans. Much of the combo material had recently come out on the Black Hawk sessions or *Someday My Prince Will Come* LPs, and it was unrealistic to expect Davis and Gil Evans to have new material for the orchestra that had previously recorded three highly successful albums: *Miles Ahead*, *Porgy and Bess* and *Sketches of Spain*. With the problems they had encountered interpreting those difficult charts in the studio, particularly *Sketches of Spain* with its alien Spanish rhythms, it was enough to hope that the orchestral players could at least play them through cleanly in a live concert setting. Once again though, Hank was on great form for the combo pieces.

Producer Teo Macero, however, thought that the concert was too good an opportunity to miss and made enquiries at Carnegie Hall to see if they had any in-house recording equipment. They had, but for a prestigious concert hall it was a bit crude and basic: a Webcor tape recorder that could record in mono, on half tracks and seven-inch reels, and a mixer that could manage up to four separate microphones. It was swiftly set up, out of sight of Davis and the musicians. Macero situated himself at the side of the stage, behind curtains, and set about making as good a recording of this major musical event as he could in the circumstances. Had it been anybody else but Miles Davis, Columbia would doubtless have refused to issue the record (*Miles Davis at Carnegie Hall*) on the grounds of sub-standard sound quality, but this concert was too good to let pass.

The concert began with 'So What', introduced by a brief flourish from the twenty-one-piece orchestra with an admittedly nervous Gil Evans having written only the opening bars. After these were played, the orchestra seemed to falter and halt rather than go on with what must have been a planned opening leading to solos. Fortunately, with great presence of mind, bassist Paul Chambers played his signature bass line and the quintet launched into a stunning combo reading. Davis and then Mobley took excellent solos, forceful, exuberant and full of invention, particularly the trumpeter's. After a short Davis solo feature, a ten-minute 'No Blues' features optimistic, up-front trumpet by the leader that is easily matched by one of Mobley's most comprehensive recorded solos. Hank keeps the momentum going on a long solo that is enthusiastically applauded as Wynton Kelly takes over for his segment. He, too, is on great form.

Considering the significance of this recording – and the latest CD issue is two discs and eighty minutes long – it is a matter of regret that it did not receive a state-of-the-art, stereo recording up to Columbia's usual standards. As it stands, it is still one of Davis' best live sessions and demonstrates once again, as the Black Hawk sets did, that Mobley was an awesomely gifted soloist and at the peak of his powers in 1961.

By this time Mobley was spending a considerable amount of time playing for other leaders in addition to Miles Davis. In addition to appearing on the record dates with Freddie Hubbard and Kenny Drew, he was recruited by trumpeter Dizzy Reece for his 1960 *Star Bright* Blue Note LP, Herbie Hancock for his *My Point of View* album, Kenny Dorham for his excellent *Whistle Stop* LP and one curiosity: a record led by two percussionists. In 1961, the drummers most in the public eye and topping the opinion polls of both critics and public were Philly Joe Jones and Elvin Jones. The two were recruited to make a record as joint leaders for Atlantic: *Philly Joe & Elvin Jones – Together*. The record is good of its kind, a display of two major percussionists working together closely, accompanying and soloing, but it is considerably enhanced by the horn section, which comprises Blue Mitchell on trumpet, Curtis Fuller on trombone and Hank Mobley on tenor sax. Wynton Kelly and Paul Chambers round out an all-star band.

Any combination of these seven players could frequently be heard on the New York club scene at this time. In fact, given the number of times they worked together in clubs, it is surprising that this appears to be one of the very few recordings on which Mobley and Elvin Jones played together. 'Brown Sugar', the longest track at fractionally under fifteen minutes, starts with a punching Mobley solo where he plays in double time frequently and uses the full range of his instrument, diving down into the depths of the lower register on more than one occasion. This, and the solos that follow by Fuller and Mitchell, make this listener wish that the drum solos had been a little shorter and all the horn solos longer. It was, though, an opportunity to exhibit the considerable percussive skills of the Joneses and a successful session, not least for the contributions of Kelly and the horn players.

The fact that Mobley was chosen to play on a record primarily to spotlight the work of two master drummers indicates that he was much more appreciated by fellow-musicians than by critics and jazz enthusiasts at this time, a point made by many commentators, at one time or another, since those days.

Although much has been made of the high-quality, near classic status, of Mobley's finest three records, made in 1960-61 (*Soul Station*, *Roll Call* and *Workout*), other discs recorded around the same time have not received their due recognition. A prime example would be Freddie Hubbard's *Goin' Up*, recorded on November 6th 1960. Very similar to *Workout*, but with Hubbard in the front line instead of Grant Green, and McCoy Tyner on piano rather than Wynton Kelly, this session fairly crackles with sparkling hard bop from the leader and his illustrious, if unrecognised as such at the time, sideman. Hubbard and Mobley fused together in much the same way that the saxophonist had found a soul mate in trumpeter Lee Morgan much earlier. Hubbard, just twenty-two at this time, was making a name for himself on the New York scene and he played in the extrovert, brassy, clean-lined style that had been pioneered in hard bop by Clifford Brown and Morgan. The combination had worked very well on *Roll Call* with a similar rhythm section and, although few if any people seem to have noticed, the music on *Goin' Up* is comparable to that session and the playing of Mobley and Hubbard just about as good.

Several factors contribute to the overall success of this album. The programme is intelligently picked for a start: two good bop lines written by trumpeter Kenny Dorham, two typical lines by Mobley, a good ballad ('I Wished I Knew') and a blues by the leader. Other factors include the compatibility of the two front-line men, the overall excellence of the rhythm section and the special chemistry and precise time sense shared by Mobley and the remarkable Philly Joe Jones. Put all these strong ingredients together and you have one great, cooking album. An infectiously swinging 'Asiatic Raes' kicks things off with Philly Joe in commanding form and Hubbard's clean, lithe lines moving easily on the surge of the rhythm section's pulse. Mobley follows with a well nigh impeccable solo segment, his phrases fitting together exactly, even if his rhythmic tinkering seems likely to throw everything out of balance at any second. Typical of the time, and of Blue Note in particular, the track ends with a stunning bass solo and exciting fours between the leader and Philly Joe. 'The Changing Scene' is one of those medium-tempo, satisfying, typically Mobley, hard bop lines that he seemed able to put together so easily, often in the studio with no prior work involved. Although the piece is obviously a 1960s-style hard bop line, the lyricism of Hubbard's solo and the relaxed, much-discussed 'round sound' of Mobley put it in a realm of its own, outside the more usual 'frameworks for solos' heard so frequently on Blue Note, Prestige and Savoy dates from this period.

Along with Lee Morgan and Donald Byrd, Hubbard was the third trumpeter who seemed to inspire Mobley so readily. Any of the tracks on *Goin' Up* demonstrate this compatibility but, in particular, the two Mobley compositions and the horn solos on the ballad 'I Wished I Knew' represent the peaks of achievement on this highly satisfying session. 'A Peck a Sec' is typical of the way Mobley could put together a piece of music to allow all the soloists to excel. This track benefits from strong solos by Hubbard and Mobley, and a particularly flowing and enjoyable one from pianist Tyner.

* * *

His tenure with the Davis quintet was certainly a period of stability for Mobley, for even when they were not working on a weekly basis, the trumpeter kept his musicians paid regularly. In spite of the uneasy relationship between the two, and the fact that Miles was certainly known to be spiky with his sidemen as well as with the press and public, it would generally seem that Davis was an easy leader to work for. Furthermore, many commentators have expressed the opinion that profound changes in Hank's style were the direct result of his association with the trumpeter. Mobley told John Litweiler in the 1970s that he and Davis would hang out together off the bandstand and sometimes they would go out to hear Ornette Coleman.

Certainly at this time, work was unusually plentiful and the sideman duties continued between leader sessions in the recording studios. One of the most significant and important recordings of this period was not under his own name: Kenny Dorham's *Whistle Stop*, recorded at Van Gelder's Englewood Cliffs studio on January 15th 1961. Mobley and Dorham had forged an impressive partnership in the original Jazz Messengers from 1954–56, when Horace Silver had described them as 'super hip', and the magic had not faded in 1961. They phrased together as though they had been playing in the same band for ten years or more and when they formed the front line on Kenny's 1961 Blue Note release the combination of Dorham's burnished gold tone and Mobley's soft 'round sound' was well nigh perfect. Add the same pulsating rhythm section that had fired up John Coltrane's *Blue Train* session in 1957 and you have a potentially explosive and musically satisfying LP.

And so it was, and it should have been recognised and promoted as such. It was not to be. Reviewing the record in the August 1961 edition of *DownBeat* magazine, at that time the leading jazz magazine worldwide in terms of circulation and influence, John S. Wilson gave it three and a half stars, a fairly good rating, but then proceeded to demolish the work. After conceding that Dorham had a 'refreshingly varied point of view as a composer', Wilson says: 'The difficulty here is that the solos do not live up to the ensembles.' He wished that Dorham had developed his composing skills to extend beyond the customary opening and closing ensembles: 'We are given a provocative promise, followed by a long wait and then return to the same thing we got at the beginning.'[2]

Perhaps somebody should have explained to Wilson that Dorham's methods were the prevalent ones in modern jazz at that time and that if he found the solos so insubstantial he should perhaps have spent his time listening only to the collective improvisation of the Original Dixieland Jazz Band and New Orleans revival outfits; there were plenty of them around then. Wilson concludes his review by saying that Dorham plays attractively but is 'almost invariably running thin towards the end'. Then he finishes with: 'Mobley has some moments of clean-lined swinging that put him in a much better light than do his usual rambling efforts.' Although my comments above about the ODJB were meant half in fun, it is worth pointing out that Wilson appeared to have a preference for older jazz from the 1930s and early 1940s and that same issue of *DownBeat* magazine contains his five- and four-star reviews of LPs by Lionel Hampton and Django Reinhardt respectively

This really sums up the problems that musicians like Mobley and Dorham had to face and the two musicians were very much alike in many ways. Both were quiet, reflective men who did not promote themselves actively, but both were accomplished, gifted soloists who composed strong jazz frameworks and had attractive, individual sounds on their instruments. Indeed Mobley's LP *Roll Call* had received a very similar review in *DownBeat* where the reviewer gave it a three-star rating (out of five) and finished up by saying that Freddie Hubbard's playing was worth hearing and it was worth watching him grow. The implication was that Mobley's album was just another run-of-the-mill release by a run-of-the-mill musician.

Critical opinion today suggests that *Roll Call* and *Whistle Stop* are among the best and most indispensable of hard bop records and the music on both of them is timeless. Jazz historians, record producers and critics have subsequently praised these discs and they are certainly no less important for being individualistic and creative statements from the broad mainstream of jazz, rather than being brash statements of the avant-garde of their day. The trouble was that, in 1961, a minor revolution in jazz was in full swing and critics and most other interested parties were busily listening to the radical statements from the avant-garde, to the exclusion of almost everything else. Ornette Coleman was making new rules and, certainly, bold and important musical statements. His music was innovative, free and remarkably refreshing, after the clichés of the boppers and the even earlier swing-era players had grown ever more stale and repetitive. The same applies to the music of Eric Dolphy and Cecil Taylor and the emerging John Coltrane Quartet, but none of that should have obscured what players such as Mobley and Dorham were doing.

Mobley was in great demand for endless sessions as a sideman and no wonder, when he had the ability to compose attractive bop lines on the spot, right there in the studio. Any disc he played on was likely to be relaxed and produce stimulating, enjoyable music. Pianist Kenny Drew's *Undercurrent* is another good example, but there are many more, too many to list here.

What Hank Mobley brought to jazz in the first four years of the 1960s was an alternative to the robust, fiercely competitive hard bop of the time – a softer, more personal sound with a unique and personal approach to rhythm. He was, in his way, the Lester Young of the hard bop era and, as with Prez in his day, everybody was attuned to a different sound and hardly anybody was listening. Eventually Lester and his alternative to the Coleman Hawkins sound were generally accepted, but it took a very long time. It took considerably longer with Mobley. In fact, to this very day he is still underrated, although gradually his work is being seen, heard and appreciated in the perspective of the long-term appreciation of classic Blue Note records.

After the euphoria of 1960 and 1961, Mobley must have suffered a traumatic event of some kind but as he was quiet, almost reclusive, and rarely agreed to speak to the jazz press or gave any other kind of interviews, we are left to speculate. The only known statement he made about this period was to John Litweiler in his 1973 interview when he said that after leaving Miles Davis, 'I was so tired of music, the whole world, man. I just went back to drugs.' And, of course, as Litweiler was quick to point out, that was exactly the wrong course of action. Hank had already served time in prison for narcotics offences and it should have been obvious to him and everybody else that the quality of his playing throughout 1960–61, both on records and live, was at an absolute peak. If he achieved that, with little or no access to harmful substances, it should have been a massive incentive to stay clean.

Little was heard from Mobley in 1962, but he led two very good quintet recording sessions on March 7th and October 2nd 1963. The March date, particularly, found him in fine form and with trumpeter Donald Byrd and an exceptionally good rhythm section comprising Herbie Hancock – just beginning to emerge as a distinctive jazz voice on piano at that time – Butch Warren on bass and Philly Joe Jones at the drums. For reasons known only to him at the time, Alfred Lion chose to take two tracks from this date and issue them with music from the October 2nd session on Hank's next Blue Note album, *No Room for*

Squares. Later he would issue two more tracks on *The Turnaround*, Hank's 1965 album, and a further two tracks sat in the vaults until the 1980s, when they were finally released posthumously on a collection called *Straight No Filter*. I will get to those later issues in due course, but because of the haphazard release of tracks from March 7th 1963, Lion failed to present what could have been one of Mobley's finest single LP collections, comparable to *Soul Station* and *Workout*.

The as-issued two-session set of *No Room for Squares* is, however, very close to the best of Mobley and will stand as such with the two tracks featuring Hancock, Warren and Philly Joe allied to four performances from October 2nd. These are sterling compositions by Hank or Lee Morgan which feature the two of them alongside pianist Andrew Hill, bassist John Ore and Philly Joe back on drums.

Litweiler suggests that a profound change in Mobley's style occurred after he left Miles Davis:

> His melodic formations grew less involved as his attention became focused on his rhythmic substructure. Now the tendency is to create a long web of shifting accents and ever changing melodic material. The structure is, if anything, more subtle than ever. Precise timing is so crucial to this delicate art, every small run or grace note has its special importance. The surface lightness and naturalness may fool you: what Mobley actually projects is some of the most intense music of our time.[3]

Whether by accident or design, Litweiler's comments are particularly appropriate to *No Room for Squares*, Mobley's first Blue Note LP after leaving Davis. The opening track, 'Three Way Split' from the October 2nd session, finds the tenor saxist playing an intriguing opening solo where he does indeed create a series of shifting accents and constantly introduces new melodic fragments. But if the emphasis is on a tighter, more economic rhythmic structure, the music loses none of its emotional directness and charm. Riding on a superb rhythmic carpet, laid out by Hill and Ore and kept precisely and accurately in check by Jones, Mobley sails along, again creating his own methods of fitting everything in by reducing the elements of his solo to the basics but playing them in his own, inimitable manner. It is an impressive achievement.

Writing for the very late, 1980s, release of *Another Workout*, Michael Cuscuna refers to Mobley's 1963 'return', saying that the music on *No Room for Squares* was different from what had gone before: 'His sound was harder and his playing had changed.' John Litweiler noted that 'Mobley credits the influence of Davis and Coltrane with the 1960s simplification of his style, for he consciously abandoned some degree of high detail in favour of concentrating his rhythmic energies.'

None of the above should surprise or disturb anyone; jazz musicians have always indulged in cross-pollination of their musical styles and Mobley was no exception, as Joe Goldberg pointed out in the sleeve note to *Soul Station*. The headlong rhythmic thrust of 'Three Way Split' and the modal playing on 'No Room for Squares' may have owed quite a bit to Miles and Coltrane, but the influence of these two giants on jazz and jazz musicians at the time was all pervasive. Trane was concentrating heavily on modal music at this time and the rhythmic energies in his quartet were at boiling point throughout most of 1961–63. Small wonder that some of his methods and ideas rubbed off on Mobley; Trane was, after all, having an effect on the playing styles of literally all of the progressive jazz musicians on the scene.

Returning to the mysterious March 7th 1963 session, I believe that had all six tracks from this date been issued on one LP and later on a CD, the resulting record would have been comparable to and well nigh as good as his three masterworks:

Soul Station, *Roll Call* and *Workout*. This was the record that never was, and we have good reason to regret Lion's strange programming activities of the time. As things stand, we are forced to consider the tracks separately, as they were presented in the sequence of the LPs on which they did come out.

'Up a Step' and 'Old World, New Imports', the two tracks that appeared on *No Room for Squares*, are both Mobley compositions. The first thing we notice is the compatibility and integration of the rhythm section. If only Hancock, Warren and Philly Joe Jones had been recruited more often together for Blue Note and worked a few club dates, they would surely have shaken down swiftly and been proclaimed as one of the greatest ever rhythm sections in jazz. The ease and fluidity of their forward drive is something to marvel at on these two selections and was almost certainly the inspiration for the inventive, hard-swinging solos produced by Mobley and his compatible front-line partner, Donald Byrd.

Byrd suffered from chronic over-exposure in the 1950s, when he seemed to be on almost every jazz LP issued by Savoy, Prestige, Blue Note and Bethlehem Records. Perhaps because of this and a certain backlash against his ubiquitousness, he has often been overlooked in critical circles when evaluating the important trumpeters of the hard bop era. As his work on the two selections from *No Room for Squares* proves conclusively, by 1963 he was one of the strongest and most original trumpeters of the hard bop school. His technique, note production, invention and originality were all impressive but these were the very points on which he was being found wanting by some critics. The trouble was that more extrovert, flamboyant trumpeters like Lee Morgan and Freddie Hubbard were catching the critics' attention and serious stylists like Byrd were largely ignored.

The speed of Byrd's execution on 'Old World, New Imports', and his soaring, high-octane trumpet style provide a suitable measure of difference between him and Mobley that enhances the work of both front-line men. Add in the velvet sweep of the swinging rhythm section and you have a contemporary modern jazz sound to treasure.

All of which is not to suggest that the other tracks on this record are inferior. Andrew Hill was at this time a much less flamboyant, more conservative pianist than Hancock, but he knew how to comp effectively and could solo well too. John Ore had a thinner sound than Butch Warren, but again he could provide a good foundation and Philly Joe was there again to drive everybody forward. And Lee Morgan on trumpet was always good value. A particularly good track here is the ballad 'Carolyn', which Morgan wrote, and on which he contributes a very well-rounded solo with Hank playing mellow counterpoint in the background. Overall, this session is almost up to the standard of the three classic sets and is pretty well indispensable to Mobley record collectors.

By 1964, however, a few prominent jazz writers were beginning to appreciate the true worth of Mobley and attempted to bring his music to the attention of a considerably larger number of people. Ira Gitler was one such person and he reviewed *No Room for Squares* enthusiastically in the August 27th 1964 issue of *DownBeat*, awarding it four and a half stars, just fractionally short of the maximum five-star (excellent) category. After writing a spirited review of the LP, Gitler made the following observation:

> Mobley has long been my choice as recipient of that overused word, underrated. Fellow musicians have realised his worth for a number of years, but others seemed oblivious to his talent. A trio of albums for Blue Note (*Soul Station*, *Roll Call* and *Workout*) should have remedied this but they did not get the recognition due to them, perhaps because they were not radical statements of the avant-garde.

Gitler was not alone in this view, although he was probably the first to voice it and one of the first to realise that there was a wide discrepancy between Mobley's talent and the degree of appreciation he was receiving. But in a sleeve note for a later Mobley album in the mid-1960s, Gitler indicated that there was a considerable (unofficial) underground appreciation society. He recalled that, at the beginning of that decade, a friend of his based in London and would return once a year to New York to stock up with the latest record releases for himself and his friends in England. One LP he purchased was *Soul Station*: 'In due course I received a letter from him, requesting that I send him two more copies of the same, one of which was for a chap who had worn the first one out. Subsequently there were impassioned calls for *Roll Call* and *Workout* as they were issued.'

Gitler remembered a British jazz bassist visiting New York at that time: 'He also spoke to me about Mobley and how many of the British musicians dug him.' According to this unnamed bass player, the appreciation had arisen from hearing Mobley play on the then newly released Miles Davis records and Hank's recent Blue Notes.

These comments by Gitler indicate how well Mobley's career could have flourished if he had received just half of the media coverage and notices and praise from the critics that Coltrane was getting at that time. Not that it was all praise; far from it: Coltrane was severely criticised throughout his career for constantly changing stylistically. As his music evolved, the commentators failed to understand it, since it was new and usually from a culture alien to the critics hearing it; so they slated it unmercifully. Mobley did not change his general style to the same extent as Coltrane or even Sonny Rollins, but he did modify his approach several times and a study of his 1950s music, compared with, say, a disc from 1961, will show that the latter is much more rhythmically focused and the sound of Hank's horn is more rounded and melodically secure. In other words, he had advanced and become a better musician, but for him it was a gradual refining of a unique and personal style.

If Mobley's sound and style have been hard to define accurately, it is probably because he appeared to combine two seemingly incompatible elements initially. Playing in the hard bop manner he took his inspiration directly from Charlie Parker but his sound seems to have been developed, to a large extent, from Lester Young. Certainly his sound calls Young to mind, but his approach, phrasing and, above all, unique rhythmic abilities, all belong to the school of bebop and hard bop. Critic and historian Leonard Feather came closest to an adequate descriptive phrase when he said: 'Hank Mobley is the middleweight champion of the tenor saxophone.' He explained his reasoning:

> That is not to say he is not to be compared (and this judgement is made in terms of size of sound as well as such values as fame, fortune and poll victories) with heavyweights like Coleman Hawkins or John Coltrane, nor is there any necessity to relate him to the tonal lightweights, headed by Stan Getz and the various artists of this school who came to prominence around the same time.[4]

Feather claimed that Mobley was the middleweight champion because his sound was 'not a big sound, not a small sound, just a round sound'. And that description had come directly from Hank himself. It was certainly the closest anybody ever came to describing the unique combination of sounds that made up his music.

Turbulence had once again invaded Mobley's life and work and in 1964 he was arrested on drugs charges and again spent time in prison. Being off the scene for a time as a result may have hampered Alfred Lion's recording or publicity plans and may well be why the four remaining tracks from the March 7th

1963 taping were shelved at that point and not released. Blue Note could have put the four selections out with two more recorded a few weeks later if Hank had been around. It may even have been Lion's plan to do just that, but the unexpected prison sentence threw everything off balance.

Mobley returned to the New York jazz scene early in 1965, renewed, fit and seemingly full of vigour, and went into the Englewood Cliffs recording studio on February 5th with a band that included old pals from the past such as Freddie Hubbard on trumpet and bassist Paul Chambers. Pianist Barry Harris was also known to Hank and the two had played together frequently in the 1950s. Billy Higgins, whose reputation for sparkling performance allied to complete reliability was growing every day, was at the drums. The record was called *The Turnaround*, a significant title as things turned out. The title track had some unusual time changes, as described by sleeve note writer Del Shields on the original LP:

> He has written a sixteen-bar blues on the outside. On the inside there are eighteen bars. Since most blues are the conventional twelve-bar structure, Hank decided to add a minor channel to the sixteen bars and thus the reason for 'The Turnaround'. So that title was inspired by a composition with an unusual eighteen-bar bridge but the wider implications of Hank's *Turnaround* concerned his different music, the tighter rhythmic structures and the somewhat harder edge to his saxophone sound.[5]

Hank's unconventional blues, 'The Turnaround', kicks off the LP because Alfred Lion then liked all his discs to begin with a soul-type, gospel-flavoured sound. After the exceptional and totally unexpected success of Lee Morgan's *The Sidewinder*, recorded in December 1963, Lion required all the musicians recording for Blue Note to come up with something along these lines to start off their albums. The track works well enough and is a foot-tapping, infectious blues that sounds as natural and unforced as all Mobley's compositions do. Hank and Freddie Hubbard both take relaxed but effectively cool solos and the rhythm section shadows them faithfully, Higgins adding commentary to spice things up.

The next two tracks on this disc are from the March 7th 1963 session and both are superior examples of Hank's art. 'East of the Village', intended as a portrait of Greenwich Village where Mobley was living at the time, is again relaxed and flows along seamlessly with Herbie Hancock and company maintaining an ultra-smooth pulse. Elements of the blues, Latin music and conventional bop swing are all present in this fascinating composition and it contains excellent solos by Mobley, Hancock and Donald Byrd. Sacha Distel's evocative ballad 'The Good Life' (recorded here before Tony Bennett made it a popular hit) is given a sensuous, breathy reading by Hank, full of warmth of expression and invention. Byrd has a tasty solo and again the rhythm section smooth his path with an exemplary, exquisitely lightweight pulse. Four tracks down and two to go, but it would be many years before the last two tracks from March 7th 1963 saw the light of day.

With four very good tracks by the Hubbard–Harris band allied to the two exceptional selections from the Byrd date, *The Turnaround* qualifies as one of Mobley's best records, on a level with *No Room for Squares* and *Hank Mobley and His All-Stars* and not very far short of *Soul Station* and *Workout*. Not the least part of its appeal is in a very slow and esoteric reading of Hank's ballad 'My Sin', which he recorded in 1955 on his first LP for Blue Note as a leader. With two very fine rhythm sections and the leader in warm, expansive mood, both versions of this piece are strong and it would be difficult to cite one as superior to the other. What is astonishing is the quality of the melodic content of the ballad. It is like a superior standard song by one of the great composers and far removed from the usual functional, if effective, compositions usually turned out by jazz musicians.

As a composer, Mobley stands out, for his originals always sound like material that we have heard many times before, even though he often 'composed' them in the studio in the middle of a recording session, with the nonchalant air of somebody churning out a pound of sausages. 'My Sin' is one of his very best ballads and a fine piece of music by any standards but so too, in a very different way, is 'Pat 'n' Chat' which rounds out this album.

Mobley told the sleeve note writer Del Shields that he was well satisfied with this LP on its completion. He continued:

> I want to get more out of my music. After you learn from the masters, you must pursue your own direction. I want to get a nice pleasant sound from the saxophone, and develop a rhythmic and swinging style.

He was about to enter a new phase of regular work and prolific recording activity, and a long spell out of his native country, but in 1965 he was just getting back into the regular tempo of life as a working musician on the New York scene.

9

Consolidation

Although some of the very best Blue Note hard bop titles came to be made early in the 1960s, before 1964 the company's general policy seemed to be to pursue the new music or what was at the time called the 'New Wave' or avant-garde. A particular problem in this period was identified by Ronald Atkins: 'many Blue Note records of the 1960s drifted along in a twilight zone; soloists still functioned as such, but in an uneasy relationship with the rhythm instruments.'[1]

Typically hard bop-oriented albums by Jackie McLean and Lee Morgan were left unreleased as the company put out the more avant-garde records, *Let Freedom Ring* and *One Step Beyond* by McLean and *Search for the New Land* by Morgan. Even so, the company held up the release of the latter for a year while they attempted to milk the sudden popular success of *The Sidewinder* by following it up swiftly with *The Rumproller*. They remained unsure whether to concentrate their efforts on the new sounds or consolidate their high-quality hard bop music by promoting it heavily; after all, it was this music that had made their name. Consequently quite a few 'standard' Blue Note releases were put on hold and did not see the light of day until the reactivation of the company in 1985.

Hank Mobley was one of the few musicians who did not present any problems to the record company. He continued to go his own way throughout the decade, oblivious as ever to the innovations of the new wave of jazz musicians. If he changed, it was on his own terms and represented merely the refinement and simplification of his old style. After the release of *The Turnaround* in 1965, he was busy with playing engagements for the next two years and indeed until the end of the decade, but for the later years the locations were very varied. On the road in the mid-sixties he was co-leader of a quintet with his old sparring partner Lee Morgan and this band was kept busy for some considerable time. The band played at Slugs, a well-frequented NYC jazz club, in June 1966, with Billy Higgins on drums and probably with Cedar Walton on piano. Mobley certainly played with Walton on several occasions at this time and they would link up again years later for a two-leader group.

Although work was plentiful, in the clubs and on record as both leader and sideman, Hank was still reserved to the point of being reclusive at all times except when on the stand and sometimes even then. In the sleeve note for Mobley's 1966 Blue Note release, *A Caddy for Daddy*, Ira Gitler wrote about going, on a wet Friday evening in March 1966, to Slugs in East New York, to hear Hank featured with the Elvin Jones Quartet. Although Gitler had been hoping to hear Mobley play, most of the solo space was taken up by a painter and part-time saxophonist called Larry Rivers. Hank was not happy and chose not to play on the selections where Rivers was featured and consequently the audience that night heard very few Mobley solos. Gitler saw this as a case of an obvious amateur taking up too much time; he should have taken a short solo and departed. But he thought that competent musicians standing in would never have inhibited Hank. Gitler also had the feeling that Hank's heart was not in his playing even when he did solo. 'He was being blocked from really getting into something.'[2]

Saxophonist and writer Dave Gelly told me a similar story. He recalled a trip to New York City to hear Mobley play. At one of the gigs, the promoter, a man known as Freddie Freeloader (the source for Miles Davis' composition on *Kind of Blue*), introduced a young woman singer and brought her on stage to play with the band. 'She was probably his girlfriend,' Dave said, 'but you could see Hank wasn't happy.' Mobley walked off the stage, clumped through the hall with heavy tread and disappeared for a good half hour. When he returned, he clumped through again, with heavy foot-stamping. With a stony face, he got back on stage and said, 'Is that chick finished yet?' Evidently that 'chick' was finished and Mobley began to play again.

If he wasn't happy with a situation he would retreat and keep away from the people he felt were bugging him. It was not in his nature to be confrontational or aggressive; he just slipped away and kept his own counsel. There are several other reported instances when this sort of thing happened and it is probably more than half the reason why Mobley seldom assumed leadership duties outside the recording studios.

It was rather different when he teamed up with Lee Morgan. The two had worked together on and off for years and Morgan's very first issued disc, arriving in the shops in 1956, just days before his first Blue Note, was *Introducing Lee Morgan, with the Hank Mobley Quintet* After that they had shared the front line in a 1959 edition of the Jazz Messengers (and one of the very best Blakey bands) and recorded and worked the clubs frequently together. Morgan employed Mobley on his Blue Note LPs *Cornbread* and *Charisma* during 1966 and also on *The Rajah* which Blue Note did not release until the 1980s. Morgan was featured on Hank's *A Caddy for Daddy* and three of the 1966 tracks that came out posthumously in 1986 as *Straight No Filter*.

Even so, a cooperative group with the trumpeter probably involved Morgan assuming most if not all the leadership duties and using Hank's name out front as a draw for the crowds. The front-line partnership worked very well in all situations and the two musicians always inspired each other to rare heights of solo playing and remained friends until Lee's tragic and untimely death in 1973, when he was shot dead by his common-law wife outside Slugs.

Yet in spite of Mobley's shyness and sometimes reclusive behaviour, he always had a desire to communicate, to reach out to the people in the audience, at least musically, and to know his fellow-musicians as well as possible. In an interview in *Melody Maker* on May 11th 1968, one of the very few he seems to have given willingly and almost enthusiastically, he said to Val Wilmer:

> Sometimes you'll see me look at the audience and shade my eyes. I always like to see who's in there. I always want to know what kind of people are they. Plus the fellows in the band. You have to get the feeling of them and the waiters and waitresses too... Over the years you get to notice things like that and I guess that's why I'm always, as you say, a leader. It's not what I want to be, to have my name upfront or anything. It's just that I'm more aware.

Whatever else he was or wasn't, Hank was always very much 'aware'. He was always aware of what was going on in jazz and the developments and innovations taking place, even if he chose not to follow them himself. He was also aware of what he was doing musically and how his unique sound and manner of phrasing were being heard by jazz aficionados and critics. In that interview with Val Wilmer he made a comparison between his style and the business of going shopping. 'It's like a grocery store, you know. We all go there and buy the same products but some people buy more than others. And then they cook them in different ways.' And it is certainly in that special, idiosyncratic method of 'cooking' that we know and appreciate the music of Hank Mobley.

Altoist Jackie McLean described Mobley as 'organically melodic'. 'And harmonically, the man is so astute. In terms of playing on the chord changes, you can't get any hipper than Hank.' Horace Silver had also said much the same thing, albeit in slightly different words. McLean also said that Hank was one of the most lyrical tenor players in the history of jazz. And he added that it was a lyricism that came naturally out of the man.

After *The Turnaround*, Hank went into the Van Gelder studio on June 18th 1965 to tape *Dippin'* and, appropriately, he had Lee Morgan and Billy Higgins with him. Harold Mabern was on piano and the bassist was Larry Ridley, another player renowned for his firm, rich sound and accurate choice of notes. It was yet another successful session. The title track, 'The Dip', is one of those, by this time obligatory, soul-type blues compositions with, as Ira Gitler points out on the liner note, a 'Spanish tinge'. Having single-mindedly invented this type of soulful opening that became familiar on post–1964 Blue Note LPs, Lee Morgan was the ideal man to stand up front with the leader yet again and offer his fiery, blues-based trumpet stylings. This piece rattles along convincingly, driven by the dexterous drumming of Higgins, whose accenting is always appropriate and complementary to the soloists. Mabern is also prominent in accompaniment and a brief, percussive solo spot. 'Recardo Bossa Nova', by Brazilian composer Djalma Ferreira, has a repetitive, insistent theme and, in this version, a light but propulsive swing from start to finish. Once again Higgins is the driving force, in tandem with Ridley's bass, but the listener is soon drawn to the sheer compatibility of Morgan and Mobley and the way they inspire each other. The composition has been a source of inspiration to dozens of jazz saxophonists over the years and it is this version that has set the style and standard. When I heard a British tenor sax soloist play this piece at a recent jazz festival, the name 'Mobley' was not mentioned, but homage was evident in every note the man played.

The ballad selected here 'I See Your Face Before Me' gets an exquisite reading with Mobley's lyricism informing every bar. It is not often chosen by jazz musicians and there are few really impressive versions by those that have attempted it, but the one by John Coltrane on his 1958 *Settin' the Pace* on Prestige and this by Mobley are outstanding. Note also Morgan's finely judged muted contribution and Mabern's stately piano solo.

Sometime in August 1965, Mobley filled an engagement on the West Coast at the popular It Club in Los Angeles. Although no details appear to have survived, it is known that Mobley's club appearances at this time were always well attended and his playing was invariably of a high standard. He often worked with Bob Cranshaw on bass and Higgins on drums in the mid-1960s and these two joined him on his Blue Note session on December 18th, which produced the album *A Caddy for Daddy*.

This record marks something of a departure, as it involved a sextet rather than Mobley's more usual quartet or quintet line-ups. Lee Morgan was back on trumpet, Curtis Fuller added on trombone and McCoy Tyner, taking a rest from the explosive John Coltrane Quartet, was at the piano. The title piece here is the usual, infectious soul blues, this time played at a fairly slow tempo and described by Ira Gitler in the album notes as 'Hank's version of rock 'n' roll', although he added that it was much more musical than the fare the idiom usually offered. Gitler noted that 'Hank told Lee what he wanted, then Lee was on his own.' Morgan leads off on the first solo and plays as though he composed the piece. And for all his tightening up of his basic style, Mobley's own solo is as earthy a blues performance as you are ever likely to encounter.

There is no ballad performance here but the programme has three attractive Mobley originals: 'The Morning After', 'Ace Deuce Trey' and 'Third Time Around' in addition to a strong piece by Wayne Shorter and the opening blues. Without being anything special or out of the ordinary, the album is another example of the high quality records that Hank was turning out consistently during this decade. Gitler suggested that far from a Caddy [Cadillac], 'this man deserves a Rolls Royce'. Better late than never perhaps, but unstinting praise such as this was still slow in coming Hank's way.

Towards the end of 1966, on November 29th, Hank was in the front line for Morgan's *The Rajah*, another sterling session that remained on the shelf until 1985, by which time the trumpeter was dead and Mobley rarely playing in public. Compositions by Cal Massey, Duke Pearson and Morgan are included, as well as two standards, and the record features Cedar Walton on piano, Paul Chambers and Billy Higgins, all of them current or ex-members of the quintet Morgan and Mobley had formed in 1966.

* * *

The year 1967 turned out to be one of change, new horizons and the beginning of a relatively happy and fulfilling time in Mobley's life. On February 24th he recorded *Third Season* with a seven-piece group, bigger than any line-up he had used before and featuring tenor sax, alto, trumpet, guitar and rhythm. The music, highly complex, yet brilliantly performed by all the musicians and especially the leader and Lee Morgan, inexplicably remained unissued until 1980. This was challenging new music, yet rooted in the hard bop style – it's not that it was free music or radically different in style from Mobley's usual material; just bigger, more complex arrangements, played with a rare degree of skill.

This set begins with 'An Aperitif'. Mobley is off on an emotive, highly charged solo from the start, his rhythmic flexibility taking full advantage of the strong support provided by pianist Cedar Walton, Walter Booker on bass and the ever reliable Higgins on drums. Writing the sleeve note for the first, 1980, issue of *Third Season*, John Litweiler made the following observation:

> The revision of his style that began in 1959 didn't exactly simplify his music; rather, he gave his improvisations a more immediately engaging surface by lightening his formed resolute lyricism with sophisticated rhythmic contrasts as a new means of balancing his structures.[3]

Litweiler suggests that this, along with Mobley's increased mastery of saxophone technique and harmony, may have inspired the vivid challenges he set himself with *Third Season*. 'It's true,' Litweiler continues, 'that far from seeming difficult, these solos fairly bubble with their inviting sparkle; within, however, they boil with rhythmic and melodic tensions.'

This then was the paradox of Mobley's music and particularly his output after 1961. He had simplified his playing by tightening up his rhythmic thrust and his solos often appeared to be more direct and basic, and yet tensions were boiling away and much more seemed to be going on in his music than was often immediately apparent.

If Mobley's compositions for *Third Season* are complex, a sterling combo, which includes Morgan, James Spaulding on alto and flute, and guitarist Sonny Greenwich, sail through them with ease. They create some wonderfully diverse hard bop solo lines while the rhythm section plays for much of the time on an equal level with the front line and creates almost as much as they do. This was Mobley working in the same style of music, as always, but raising it to new and ever more expressive heights. This session might lack the more immediate appeal and easy swing of *Soul Station* and *Workout* but, on the other hand, it offers a new freshness and an injection of further sophistication into an old jazz form.

In March 1967, Mobley travelled out of the USA for the first time to play an engagement at Ronnie Scott's jazz club in London, where he was well received and appreciated by local audiences.[4] His performances were so successful that the engagement was extended to seven weeks. His only complaint was that he was somewhat homesick after a time; he claimed that he missed America, Dizzy Gillespie, Art Blakey and Miles Davis, although not necessarily in that order. After London, he set off on a hectic tour of Europe and then returned to the United States and continued to work at a furious pace.

On May 26th he recorded *Far Away Lands*, another strong session and yet another set that was left on the shelf until the 1980s. This time the trumpeter was Donald Byrd.

Their partnership works extremely well, as always, and this session sounds for all the world like a throwback to the Mobley records of the mid to late 1950s. With the leader's compositions 'The Hippity Hop' and 'Bossa for Baby', and Donald Byrd's 'Soul Time', this is basic bop and blues the way they used to do it and there is no reliance on complex arrangements or tightly structured rhythm. It is a very attractive programme but straight-ahead in an old style and this fact might, for once, provide a clue as to why Blue Note left it on the shelf. Lion quite likely thought it did not accurately display Mobley's playing at that time as represented by albums like *A Caddy for Daddy*.

A similar fate had been suffered by Jackie McLean's more traditional recordings in the 1960s although he embraced the 'New Wave' much more readily and enthusiastically than either Mobley or Byrd. Blue Note tried, with varying degrees of success, to balance production of music that was at the cutting edge of the current free jazz of the mid-1960s with the more traditional hard bop for which the label had become deservedly famous. As more and more of its regular musician leaders began to flirt with more contemporary sounds, it often must have seemed to the directors that the newer style of music should take priority. And if this new music was all released it was inevitable that more traditional material would have been put on hold. Unfortunately, with the changes of style, management, and various other factors, much of it was forgotten and left to collect dust in the vaults.

Hank continued to work hard, record and play live dates. But, as 1968 dawned, music was changing; rock was in the ascendancy and jazz fusion was just around the corner, heralding hard times and scuffling for even the best jazz musicians. Good, straight-ahead jazz was not reaching the public at this time and over the next decade it would go into serious, but fortunately not terminal, decline. Mobley was about to receive a call to work again in Europe and this time it would be an extended stay, to some extent broadening his experience of life.

10

Europe

Early in 1968, January 19th to be precise, Hank went into the Van Gelder studio in Englewood Cliffs to make what was to be his most commercial recording: *Reach Out*. Woody Shaw was on trumpet and at that time considered, correctly, to be one of the best and most original of the up-coming young trumpet players in modern jazz. A good rhythm section was lined up with Lamont Johnson on piano, along with old mates Bob Cranshaw and Billy Higgins, and George Benson on guitar. First up is 'Reach Out, I'll Be There', a rock 'n' roll hit of the time but, as writer Nat Hentoff points out in the sleeve note, from the very start 'there is a firm, blues-coloured jazz foundation, propelled by George Benson. Hank starts building and is, as he shows here, a "speaking" kind of player. He's always telling a story.'

What is a fairly bland but catchy tune is here somehow elevated to the realm of blues standard with the playing of Mobley, Benson and Shaw and the solid path laid out by the rhythm section. It is a very good example of how to make something worthy out of very little. 'Up Over and Out' is a more conventional Mobley-type line and the faster tempo seems to suit both him and the rhythm section. The leader and Higgins are outstanding on this track, which swings mightily from start to finish. The LP was a good one overall, if perhaps not quite up to Hank's usual, very high standards and it appears to be the only time that he chose, or was persuaded, to go for a certain measure of 'pop' appeal with 'Reach Out'. There was also, for good measure, 'Goin' Out of My Head', another pop hit tune which seems to indicate that Hank was deliberately going for a more pop-orientated audience. With his warm, lyrical solo on this track, however, he was certainly unlikely to offend his more straight-ahead jazz fans. *Reach Out* remains a one-shot, never-repeated flirtation with rock and Hank was to return to more conventional jazz material for his next discs.

In spring 1968, he received a telephone call from his old friend, trombonist/arranger Slide Hampton in Paris, who asked if Mobley would come over and take his place in a band. It was, according to John Litweiler, the start of one of the happiest periods in his life, although it began somewhat badly. There was a strike in Paris when Mobley arrived there in May after working at Ronnie Scott's Club in London. He told Litweiler in 1973:

> Soon as I got there they had the fight at the Sorbonne. The whole city was on strike; you couldn't get a taxi, you couldn't get nowhere. The train left me way out in the desert, it seemed, and I had to work at the Chat-qui-Pêche that same night. Slide Hampton's niece, I think, came to pick me up, finally. People going around with rifles, all that kind of stuff. I didn't have to go 4,000 miles – I saw all this at home. I checked into the hotel and just stayed there and looked out the window.

Typical of Mobley and very similar to the way he tended to behave at home in the USA, not mixing but staying in his car during club intervals or refusing to play if there was somebody he didn't respect in the band, he took the non-risk way in Paris and stayed quietly in his hotel room until things began to get back to normal.

It was not long, however, before he was meeting and then hanging out with tenor saxist Johnny Griffin and drummer Art Taylor, both of whom were working and living in Paris at that time. The many job opportunities, the appreciation of the audiences and the almost complete lack of racism compared to the USA led to several American jazz musicians living and working in Paris and other friendly European cities at that time. 'In Paris there's a lot more communication between musicians than in the States. An American in Paris is a long way from home,' Mobley told Litweiler. Kenny Clarke, the drummer, lived just outside the city and all the American musicians would meet at a club called the Living Room in the centre of Paris It was there that Hank first met one of his boyhood heroes, Don Byas.

Mobley remembered meeting up one night with Paul Gonsalves, Byas, and Archie Shepp. The four saxophonists left the club together and ended up sitting somewhere with a bottle on the floor. Hank told the story to Litweiler in 1973:

Everybody said, we ain't going to drink anything now. Course I know when Paul and Don start drinking they might go crazy. We were at a round table talking shop – that was one of the most beautiful nights of my life – and we had to stay up for Paul; he had a habit of missing the bus. At six or seven in the morning we got Paul on the bus, then we went back to Archie's crib, and we still aren't finished. Now we had a cooking contest. I started off making breakfast. Don baked a cake, and Archie made lunch. When I got home that afternoon, I was, whew . . . Those were good days. I'd say, 'This reminds me of how it should be.'

Considering Hank's quiet, almost reclusive nature, this sojourn in Paris showed him in his most outgoing, expansive light, a happy state of things not to be repeated, unfortunately. And considering, too, the appreciation of European audiences for jazz and the respect they had for it, he might have fared better had he settled there or somewhere else in Europe for several years, as Dexter Gordon, Bud Powell, Don Byas, Johnny Griffin, Kenny Clarke and a host of others did. Ultimately, Mobley stayed in Europe for two years. It was a longish time but five or six would probably have been even better given his personality and character. The pace of life was slower, racial tensions were almost unheard of and audiences listened to jazz in appreciative silence. It was just the sort of environment that, if he had experienced it for long enough, could have set Mobley up for a successful career and many years of good living.

There were, however, many pleasures to come before he went home to America. After working in the more usual and expected parts of Europe such as Rome and Munich, Hank set off to play in Poland, Hungary and Yugoslavia. 'You'd have such a rapport with the people,' he reported, and he found time and again that European audiences were there to listen to the music rather than chatter noisily. Talking about the venues in Eastern Europe he said: 'All those places were like the Metropolitan Opera House.'

He had worked in the USA with what really amounted to a repertory company (Freddie Hubbard/Lee Morgan/Kenny Dorham/Cedar Walton/Jackie McLean/Billy Higgins) and found that system conducive to his most creative musical moments, but the set-up in Europe was, of necessity, with local pick-up rhythm sections and anybody who could really play. 'Unlikely combinations were the rule,' he said later. This was alien to him musically and to his unique manner of integrating with fellow-musicians, and it may have been a reason why he did not stay longer in Europe. Yet he seems to have been happier and much more outgoing during this period than at any other time and he actually consented to an interview with Val Wilmer published in *Melody Maker* in May 1968. This suggested a change from his reclusive attitude in the early 1960s when Dave Gelly, in America to hear jazz and following him from gig to gig, found that he spent his interval times hunched up in his car, smoking and, by implication, avoiding contact with journalists and members of the audience.

Gelly had reported that Hank had only one gig a week in 1963, and 'whatever else came along'. Gelly followed him about for several weeks and never missed a gig, but he noted that there were not many to miss. The image that stuck in his mind from those times was not so much the music, wonderful as it was, but Hank outside the famous Five Spot Café in New York. 'Whenever I listen to his records now I see that figure slumped in the driving seat of a parked car in St Mark's Place.'[1]

So positive progress had been made in the intervening five years. In 1963 Mobley was playing at his absolute peak of creativity, had only one gig a week, and avoided all human contact when he was not actually playing on the bandstand. By 1968 he had recorded dozens of albums, must have been making good money, was playing well, was in the middle of an extended European tour where he was rapturously received and was feeling, by his standards, positively extrovert. No more crouching in cars at intervals; he was actually talking to a British journalist.

Wilmer found him superficially laconic and prepared grudgingly to admit to the influences he had absorbed. This was where he made the comparison with a grocery shop and people buying different foods and cooking them in different ways. Too modest to accept that he had been a major influence himself, he said: 'But I think as far as copying – some of the other cats may have overtones, but if they copied completely, they'd lose their complete self.'[2]

The character of Hank Mobley and the person he had become by May 1968 began, slowly, to emerge during that interview with Wilmer. Comparing what he was playing at that time with his earlier music, he said that the themes were completely different. 'I like to play anything that makes sense and that moves and is not restricted,' he said. 'You might say "half free", "three-quarters free", something like that.' Then he continued, stressing that improvisation itself did not mean complete freedom: 'You have a twelve-note thing, chords, scales and you improvise on those scales and things. It's so restricted that way, but if you change them all around and try to reach the people also, that's like freedom with a little restriction.'

At this point he gave what Wilmer described as one of his rare smiles. But it can be seen from the above quote that Hank was merely doing what his uncle had advised him to do, all those years ago: if you're with someone that plays loud, you play soft, etc. In other words always do something different, be original, be yourself and present music to the audience that is yours and yours alone and is played a little differently to the other tenor players. And this, perhaps, is the real key to understanding Mobley and coming to terms with the fact that he was never a big, commercial name, even in the world of jazz. It is, surely, all too easy to say he was unfashionable and lacked the currently popular big, hard sounds that Rollins, Coltrane and Griffin had. Mobley was so busy being different and deliberately playing in opposite directions to the other leading instrumentalists that he probably engineered his own obscurity, or part of it. Certainly his records sold well over the years and still do to this day, and if he had used slightly more orthodox approaches to rhythm, harmony and sound and been a little less introverted, he could well have become one of those big names. He surely had enough talent as a musician.

The other factor contributing to Mobley's relative obscurity was his sheer indifference to everything that was going on around him for prolonged periods of time. Talking about his way of playing and that of other people, in particular his friend Archie Shepp, Hank said: 'They have one direction to play, I have another. I don't think their's is complete and mine certainly isn't. It's the same thing with Jackie [McLean], we're all together in that we're all trying to find something. None of us are completed.' He told Wilmer, revealingly: 'You have to be an extrovert to stay in front and I'm an introvert for most of the time. Sometimes I look on the worst side of things but it really depends what part of the day it is.'

Although Mobley presented himself as someone 'almost ashamed to admit to taking an interest in anything outside the daily round', Val Wilmer remained unconvinced. She pointed out that he sometimes wrote down his personal philosophies in his spare time, 'a rare pursuit for a jazzman of the Mobley inclination', and summed him up neatly in the following paragraph:

> Mobley's success has been limited by the sales of his Blue Note albums and he feels that the market has frequently been flooded by too much of his work. His apparently indifferent attitude to business and, at times, the music itself, has also held up his progress . . . He is a perceptive person at heart.

Val Wilmer told me recently that her best description of Mobley would be 'fragile'. She said other musicians treated him as fragile too. 'They looked out for him.'

This then was the enigma of Mobley in 1968. Whether his plan was eventually to make a name for himself by being radically different and it misfired due to his introverted nature and frequent periods of indifference to what was going on around him, we shall probably never know for sure. But there is certainly more to discover by examining the rest of his productive and enjoyable sojourn in Europe before turning to the events that began to change his life after his return to the USA.

While he was still in London, playing to audiences that gave him often rapturous receptions at Ronnie Scott's in Soho, Hank must have frequently wondered why his music seldom, if ever, received the same appreciation back home. The enthusiasm of club owner Ronnie Scott was not difficult to understand; Mobley had long been one of his favourite tenor players and the comparatively recently recorded *Soul Station*, was Scott's favourite Mobley disc. The reactions of London, Paris and Munich audiences must have indicated to Hank that he was much more than the jobbing tenor saxman that everybody in the USA seemed to consider him. If nothing else, his stay in Europe proved his versatility and adaptability once and for all. Until the European trip he had never worked with European rhythm sections and, indeed, was more into working regularly with a constant clique of musicians than many other soloists were.

The years spent in Europe represented one of the few extended periods in his life when Mobley was both relatively content and musically fulfilled, at least in terms of the amount of work he was getting. But his arrival in London in the spring of 1968 was less than auspicious. According to journalist John Fordham, Mobley arrived in London from the USA, sick, broke and physically worn out. He had, according to the same source, telephoned fellow-musician Ronnie Scott from Heathrow in the small hours of the morning. Mobley had played at the Scott Club the previous year with great success and now turned to his friends in London for help. Scott's response was immediate and compassionate: he dressed swiftly, drove out to the airport to collect Hank, took him back to his club and made sure that his accommodation and other needs were met until he got back on his feet.

This was typical of Scott; he would go to almost any lengths to ensure the comfort of musicians who played at his club and it is perhaps unfortunate that three of the musicians he admired most, Stan Getz, Lucky Thompson and Hank Mobley, caused him the most problems. Getz and Thompson were great musicians with difficult personalities and their antics have been documented elsewhere, but Hank was quiet, reserved and no problem to anybody when he was on the bandstand, yet thoroughly unreliable and unpredictable at all other times. His main problem seems to have been not showing up at gigs with little or no explanation, which may well have been due to his dependence on hard drugs at certain key times in his career. This may, incidentally, have provided Wayne Shorter with an opportunity as he first appeared with the Jazz Messengers in the early 1960s when Hank started to miss gigs.

In fact, Hank had been booked, through a Dutch agency, to appear at Ronnie Scott's as early as October 1965, at the original club in Gerrard Street, Soho. Scott and his business partner Pete King had driven to Heathrow on that occasion to pick up the tenorist, but he did not arrive. King later reported that Hank had illness in the family and passport problems but Art Blakey could have told them that Hank had failed to show up for gigs on more than one occasion.

In any event, Mobley's highly successful seven week season at the Scott Club in the spring of 1967 had made up for any previous difficulties and Scott continued to admire Hank greatly as a musician. Mobley was able to turn to Scott when things were going badly and was not let down. And he was able to repay the generosity he had received with inspired playing for much of his next engagement at the club. Mobley opened at Scott's new place for one month on April 22nd 1968. He was fixed up with Tubby Hayes' regular rhythm section of the time: pianist Mike Pyne, bassist Ronnie Mathewson and drummer Tony Levin. A contemporary report in *Melody Maker* suggested that the first night was hardly a great success but, Bob

Dawburn added: 'if he didn't catch fire on the opening night, there is no doubt that he will – and lovers of first-class modern tenor playing should be there when he does.'[3] No surprises there. In fact, it would have been remarkable if Mobley had fused with an unfamiliar section on the first night. At that time he was used to playing only with top notch New York rhythm sections.

During her interview with him, Val Wilmer suggested that for almost twenty years he had been at the centre of one after another New York clique. She pointed out that he regularly recorded with Lee Morgan, Freddie Hubbard, Bill Hardman, Charles Tolliver, Cedar Walton and Billy Higgins. She could well have added Jackie McLean, Philly Joe Jones and John Hicks. Mobley was one of a select three or four musicians who recorded regularly for Blue Note every few months. But where Horace Silver always brought in a regular quintet that he took out on the road and Jimmy Smith used a trio that he kept together for years, Hank always worked in the Blue Note Records method of musical repertory. The company had a nucleus of musicians who came in to record as leaders and the same people became sidemen for each other. Hank seemed happy to follow this method of working and consequently found himself playing in clubs and at other gigs alongside the musicians he had recently been working with in the studios.

Responding to Wilmer's observation, he replied:

> I guess you could call it a clique, but recording is sort of like a business. Personal life is different but these are the most business-like kind of groups to work with, the people you can rely on to work all kinds of jobs. Bass players I like are people like Walter Booker, Cecil McBee, Paul Chambers; these guys are the mainstay.

This indicates that, although he did not work with a regular group for any length of time, he chose his companions very carefully, assessing their ability before linking up with them. Wilmer concluded that he showed little emotion on the bandstand, and preferred to work with the other musicians rather than for the people who paid to hear him. Yet, she said, 'he pays the audience more attention than you'd imagine from a cursory glance.'

More and more, if gradually, we begin to see from his music and behaviour from the mid-1950s to the late 1960s that Mobley's agenda was much more planned and astute than a casual appraisal might suggest. He went out of his way to be different and do things that other tenor men did not do and yet he was very much aware of audience reaction and played up to it in his own oblique manner. His casual demeanour off stage and avoidance of social intercourse on all but a very few occasions indicates a quiet, placid, introverted man who did not seek fame and fortune but was quietly determined to make his mark as a highly original musician, on his own terms and at his own pace. In this at least, and on those self-imposed terms, he surely succeeded.

In addition to the engagement at Ronnie Scott's club in Soho, Ronnie's partner and business manager, Pete King, had been able to line up other work for Hank including a trip to the north of England to play at Club 43 in Manchester.

Following that, Mobley's first dates on the Continent started him off on what was to prove an extended stay. He would play in any size of group from a trio upwards and linked with likely American expatriate colleagues such as Dexter Gordon, Kenny Clarke and Don Byas, as well as rather unlikely ones such as Ornette Coleman and Ben Webster. In Paris he had engagements at Le Chat-qui-Pêche, with Philly Joe Jones behind him on the drums. No doubt the presence and stimulating percussion provided by Jones gave him confidence in unknown and unusual environments. He played frequently in

Italy and, more surprisingly perhaps, Yugoslavia, but always with local rhythm sections; so he and they had to adapt quickly to make an impact. All available reports, however, indicate that Hank was successful wherever he went and continued to be so for the duration of his stay in Europe. While Hank was in London, there was also an All Star Jazz Concert at the Royal Festival Hall, where Mobley and Phil Woods played, although Bob Dawbarn, in *Melody Maker* (which had sponsored the concert), again found Hank's playing 'slightly disappointing'.

One of the major benefits of Hank's European work was the link-up with Philly Joe Jones who had relocated to London in 1967 and then to Paris in 1969. After they began playing regularly together Hank never looked back. Soon after completing the gig at Scott's club in May 1968, Mobley and Philly had begun jamming together in London. The two were very close friends and this continued until Jones' death in 1982.

After a prolonged absence from recording studios, Hank finally got the opportunity to record for Blue Note again on July 12th 1969 at Studio Barclay in Paris. *The Flip* was produced by Francis Wolff, who flew to Paris to supervise it. By this time, Alfred Lion was no longer in the picture and Blue Note Records had been sold to Liberty. Even so, this was like old times and the session was not far removed in spirit from a typical Blue Note recording at Englewood Cliffs. A major factor was the availability of Philly Joe Jones, along with another friend, trombonist Slide Hampton, as well as Dizzy Reece, the slightly eccentric but often brilliant Jamaican-born trumpeter who had moved across the Atlantic from Britain to the USA around 1959 and engaged Hank to play on one of his first Blue Note LPs as a leader. Perhaps this was Hank belatedly returning the favour, albeit nine years on. At any rate, it made for a highly compatible trio of players: two fine front-line companions and one of the drummers that Hank enjoyed playing with most.

I've listened closely to this record on many occasions, trying to decide whether or not it differs in a marked manner from Mobley's American releases but, in truth, it really doesn't. The pianist, Vince Benedetti, is not quite a soloist in the Sonny Clark, Wynton Kelly, Barry Harris, McCoy Tyner, Cedar Walton league but then very few others, even in the USA at that time, could match that criterion and he certainly comps well and supportively throughout. The same comments apply to bassist Alby Cullaz, who swings along adequately, keeping the time steady without ever posing a threat to Paul Chambers, Walter Booker or Bob Cranshaw. In fact the general ambience and musical content on the session is up to Englewood Cliffs *circa* 1963–68 standards and if it was played blindfold to Mobley enthusiasts for the first time, I seriously doubt that they could tell that it ws not a Van Gelder recording.

The CD kicks off with the title track which is, in effect, a typical soul-type blues, and Hank plays the sort of solo that was very much his thing at this time. Reece's solo is more quirky and eccentric than even he usually came up with, but it does provide a rather good contrast with Mobley's straight-ahead offering. Then Hampton brings everything back to ground level with another in-the-tradition type solo.

The entire record sounds like a Mobley Blue Note from around 1965–66, a bit earlier than it actually was, but that may have been due to the fact that Mobley was unfamiliar with Benedetti and Cullaz, and reuniting on record with Philly Joe after four years separation. These factors would have led to the tenor saxist writing and playing in a slightly simplified style and putting on hold the innovative departures he had inaugurated with discs like *Third Season*. As to 'Feelin' Folksy', this track is even more like an earlier Mobley original, similar to his late-1950s, early-1960 output. The presence of Philly Joe at something near his best and, to a much lesser extent, the erratic but often brilliant Reece, is crucial to the success of this disc.

Recording away from home with unfamiliar musicians on foreign territory could have been a disaster for a man who had worked at and refined the repertory system, ensuring that he always got the best of support from his sidemen. It is also the case, I believe, that although Hank often worked with pick-up rhythm sections during his years on the continent of Europe, it was a situation that he had to adapt to in order to survive; he was never at his best without three or four familiar faces in the line-up. This was, I feel, an important factor in the way he was able to fabricate and develop and refine his very individualistic sound and style, but I will investigate the thesis more thoroughly in the next chapter.

The surprise about *The Flip* is that Hank could, seemingly easily, replicate a typical Blue Note set thousands of miles away and with two unfamiliar colleagues. In the liner notes to this release Leonard Feather wrote that when he went to France on a transcontinental jazz concert tour, he had run into Hank in a Paris nightclub. 'After sitting in with the resident combo and playing with more assurance and conviction than ever, he told me he had been in Europe since the previous March.'[4] Feather seemed surprised that Hank was both playing extremely well in Europe and able to produce a first-class album there, although it is the manner of his writing rather than his actual words that conveys this impression. But it is certain that Mobley had adapted very well and settled into the European way of life by July 1969.

A month later, Hank was busily working and recording with Archie Shepp who, although an uncompromising exponent of the avant-garde style of the day, seems to have become a close friend of Mobley at this time. Shepp was in Paris recording for the BYG label with groups of various sizes, some of which included Mobley. Hank and Shepp improvised together on 'Oleo' and 'Sonny's Back'. Once again, the inventive and impressive Philly Joe Jones is heard at the drums.

Another benefit of Mobley's Continental months was meeting up with Dexter Gordon, at that time the most famous and well respected of all the Americans in Europe. The two became friends and Gordon nicknamed Mobley 'Hankenstein'. At that time, Dexter was appearing frequently at the Jazzhus Montmartre club in Copenhagen, a haven for jazz enthusiasts and musicians. There was a pleasant, warm ambience at this venue, soon to become world-famous, with jazz every week and American stars such as Don Byas, Brew Moore, Ben Webster and Gordon featured regularly. There was also a first-rate house rhythm section of pianist Kenny Drew, drummer Al 'Tootie' Heath and Scandinavian teenage wonder bassist, Niels-Henning Ørsted Pedersen. At this stage, Hank must have lost contact for a time with Philly Joe, although it is known that they toured extensively together. However, tapes exist of Mobley at the Montmartre club, with Drew, Heath and Pedersen, playing familiar material such as 'Workout', 'Third Time Around', and 'Up Over and Out'. There is much to enjoy on these tapes which I was fortunate enough to acquire during research for this book. Mobley sounds at ease with this sterling rhythm section behind him and, in spite of the relatively lo-fi, much of the lively ambience of the club is caught for posterity. The recording balance is poor – unsurprising if this was an amateur, illegal taping – but the over-recorded drums do give an indication of the sound and atmosphere in a small jazz club with Tootie Heath in inspired form throughout a long gig.

Mobley's solos come tumbling out unimpeded, his stream of inventive phrases almost tripping over each other at fast tempi. On 'Up Over and Out' he expands considerably on his studio-recorded version of this tune on the *Slice of the Top* LP. Here he has twice as long to make his statements and, typically, the more generous time frame is no hindrance as it is to so many soloists; Hank is continually inventive for about ten minutes. Drew and Heath provide constantly stimulating support and, no doubt, so does Pedersen; unfortunately he is largely inaudible except in solo.

Other delights include hearing Hank play Thelonious Monk, compositions, an intriguing glimpse of what might have been if the two had ever recorded together. (There is, I believe, one track on a compilation of rare Monk pieces of the two but the sound is so poor it cannot be enjoyed or studied properly.) These sessions from the Jazzhus Montmartre kick off with Monk's 'Rhythm-a-Ning' and later in the programme Hank tackles 'Blue Monk' with highly enjoyable results.

'Third Time Around', another favourite theme that Mobley had kicked around more than once, is given an extended workout on the tapes. It is fascinating to hear him building slowly and logically over a very long solo segment, as he had done with 'Up Over and Out'. It appears possible to hear his thought processes at times as he weaves variation after variation on a simple theme, only very occasionally pausing to collect his thoughts or, very rarely indeed, repeating himself while he waits for inspiration to return. Ninety per cent of the time, he provides a constant stream of invention, newly minted phrases pouring out uninterrupted. Drew's piano interlude is much shorter and he occasionally appears bereft of ideas, which only throws into relief the amazingly prolific invention of the saxophonist.

The difference between these performances and various of the same pieces that have appeared on LPs and CDs is almost as great as that between LPs and the old 78 rpm records which they superseded. Here Hank can stretch out, with solos that frequently extend to fifteen or more minutes, and sound relaxed and in constant command throughout. It is also instructive to hear him improvising on material that is less familiar. A long reading of 'Summertime' is followed by Sonny Rollins' 'Airegin' and there are sterling interpretations of Kenny Dorham's 'Blue Bossa' and the ballad 'Alone Together'. 'Summertime' has more than a few traces of John Coltrane's approach to this piece, which proves that his pervasive influence was, at times, too strong even for the highly independent Mobley. 'If I Were a Bell' was probably chosen because Hank remembered playing it regularly with Miles Davis.

Most interesting of all, though, are the two Thelonious Monk compositions. 'Rhythm-a-Ning' is taken at a fairly fast clip with Mobley varying the timbre considerably between the various sections. When he gets into his stride, the quirky contours of Monk's theme are taken by the scruff of the neck and shaken to fit the saxophonist's concept. It remains recognisably Monk but at the same time is typical Mobley, his relaxed tempo and nonchalant negotiation of the chord changes all going to make this sound like a one of Mobley's Blue Note compositions. It is a trick that few, if any, others have been able to bring off when playing Monk.

Even that most personal anthem of Thelonious, 'Blue Monk', is treated to an idiosyncratic, personal interpretation that is light-years away from the average reading. Hank begins by playing half of the opening theme statement and leaves his pianist to finish it. Then he plays the melody through, altering a note here and there, and launches into a long, protracted improvisation where he gradually but irresistibly begins to make the composition his own, for the duration of this performance at any rate. Monk's blues is recognisable throughout this partial transformation process; the trick is that it sounds also like a Mobley line throughout while retaining its own identity. After the piano solo Hank's next chorus moves further away from Monk's line and then Pedersen takes a short bass solo. Mobley toys with Monk's blues chords, twists and turns and finally ends with Miles Davis' sign-off piece, known simply as 'The Theme'.

A long workout on 'If I Were a Bell' confirms that Mobley could expand on a familiar theme that he had used previously on record and come up with an entirely different set of variations, keeping the invention going without flagging for ten to fifteen minutes and sometimes more. And the long version of this selection heard on the tape is edited! Coltrane would often stretch out for thirty to sixty minutes on one selection towards the end of his life and Mobley appears to have worked along similar lines on his live appearances. The obvious conclusion to draw, of course, is that only a handful of soloists, such as Coltrane and Mobley could adopt this practice and keep the audience in rapt attention throughout.

Also included on the Montmartre tapes is 'Workout', the ferocious, headlong blues that had been a highlight of one of Mobley's very best LPs in 1961. In the late 1960s, not a lot had changed except that his control of the saxophone in all registers seems to have improved. There are no squeals or rough edges here, although it should be said that the raw, energetic playing on the record was part of the reason for its success. And the performance on disc sounded wonderfully spontaneous, each phrase newly minted; on this live performance you do get the impression that Hank had played this selection many times over and was merely going through the motions part of the time. Occasionally he hits on a new idea and begins to develop it, but then he slips back to repetition and pet runs, over-familiarity probably being the culprit.

Overall, though, these tapes are invaluable because they show us Mobley in a live setting, stretching out and with little editing; all of his live appearances on record with Miles Davis were severely edited and even where most of his solos have been restored on later releases (such as the Blackhawk CDs), this was Hank the sideman; the Montmartre tapes give us the leader in full flow and allow us a rare insight into his capacity to improvise at great length.

This is, though, a bootleg tape and the music has never been commercially released, an oversight that should be rectified as soon as possible by whoever owns the master tapes. It was recorded in a smart and well-organised jazz club, so perhaps there are professional-quality tapes lurking about somewhere. If not, and if indeed these were illegal, even the bootleg tapes could surely get clearance and be cleaned up and released.

Dexter Gordon, himself a regular on the bandstand at the Montmartre club in this period, well understood the value of Mobley's music. He said of his friend:

> Hank is definitely the 'middleweight champ' of the tenor. And that is meant to be as high an estimation as I can make of his playing . . . and it doesn't imply any limitation in his talent whatsoever; with that round sound and medium tone, he plays as hip as any tenor player around.

11

The Enigma of Hank Mobley

So far, this study of Hank Mobley has revealed certain key points about him but they do not give the complete picture. We know that he was shy and reticent with all but a few intimate family members and also that he sought to fashion a unique jazz style by always doing the opposite to, or at least something different from, what all the other tenor players were doing. We can safely assume, from Hank's words, and Val Wilmer's observations, that he was more aware of and more interested in the audience reactions to his music than he ever really indicated in public. How, though, do we explain a unique sound that was popular enough to sell thousands of LPs and CDs and yet a failure to achieve recognition and respect with the jazz community in general throughout his lifetime? For more clues I believe it will be instructive to look at his methods of working and the dependence that I believe he had on the sidemen and colleagues with whom he worked.

The first claims about the importance of rhythm section colleagues to Mobley's music came in an article by Michael James, back in October 1961,[1] long before it became clear that his career would never really blossom beyond the confines of the recording studios and a few favourite club haunts. James made the point that in a music where improvisation in a group context played a major role, any soloist's efforts would stand or fall on the degree of cooperation he receives from his rhythm section. James continued: 'We should not be surprised, then, if cliques grow up, loose associations of players having certain principles and aims in common.' James was making much of the fact that the objectives of a musician like Mobley could be accurately judged by the company he kept. He also pointed out that Mobley's rhythm section associates over the years had been such people as Art Taylor, Horace Silver, Art Blakey, Philly Joe Jones, Paul Chambers, Doug Watkins, Kenny Drew and Wynton Kelly. This was, of course, before Hank began to lose contact with Blakey, Silver and Drew and before he formed similar but telling associations with Cedar Walton, Billy Higgins and John Hicks. It was the same pattern as before, with Mobley establishing a very strong rapport with Billy Higgins, that saw the drummer appear on almost all of his LPs from 1965 onwards.

Michael James' main point was that the rhythm section players he mentioned tended to impinge on what had previously been thought to be the sole province of the front-line soloist. He suggested that if we listen to Mobley's improvisations without paying very much attention to what the drummer, pianist or bass player are doing, the charm of those choruses will elude us. This is, of course, true of all jazz soloists to some extent but, as James acknowledged, more so with Mobley because 'rhythmically he begins where most of his less gifted contemporaries leave off'.

James gave the example of 'Touch and Go' from the two-trumpet sextet date of November 25th 1956. The beginning of Mobley's solo on this track sounds as if it had been patched in at random without any attention being paid to what Lee

Morgan, Donald Byrd and the rhythm section had been doing before him. Then, as usual, Mobley adapts and plays at his own pace, fits all his phrases in neatly and creates an integrated sequence with the rhythm section even though he is playing in a highly unconventional manner, as the majority of jazz soloists would see it. He cuts across bar lines, makes the lines breathe to suit himself and generally manages to give the illusion that he is playing in a conventional manner. As Michael James put it in his *Jazz Monthly* article:

> Mobley distinguishes himself not so much by his ability to create a cohesive solo while ignoring the conventional four- and eight-bar phrase unit . . . as by the melodic concentration and extreme rhythmic richness of his playing. This is why awareness of the context in which his solos occur is vital to the understanding of his music. The steady metric pulse created by the bass line and the drummer's cymbal beat throws the curious convolutions of his phrases into relief as the piano commentary and the extra figures and accents devised by the drummer help to balance and underline them. The upshot is that almost any of his solos is marked out by a succession of tensions and resolutions.

'Touch and Go' is indeed a good example of Mobley's fragmented, almost arbitrary approach to a piece of music, yet 'Double Whammy' from the same 1956 record has him coming in after the initial theme statement in a less than typical and highly conventional manner and fashioning a solo that Lester Young or Stan Getz would have been proud of. Mobley changed from moment to moment, depending on how the mood took him, and could play conventionally if he wanted to. The point is that he rarely wanted to, and always sought to be different to distinguish himself from the rest of the tenor saxophonists on the scene. He had a unique approach to rhythm and a tendency always to manage to fit in everything that he wanted to play, no matter how much he chopped up the basic rhythm patterns of the section to do it. These features of his playing may have had their beginnings in 1954 when he became the saxophonist in the original Jazz Messengers.

When Horace Silver and Art Blakey got together to form the cooperative unit that was the Messengers, it was a new band and a new concept; bebop as played by Bird, Diz and others was becoming somewhat stale and predictable. Blakey and Silver stripped bebop down to its essential blues-based components and, with an emphasis on fast, furious, keep-up-or-die rhythms, began what came to be called 'hard bop'. In those days it was the start of a new variation on modern jazz with only Max Roach, Clifford Brown and a very few others working along the same lines, and soloists had to be fleet and agile to keep to the rhythmic timetable or, as one critic put it, be hurled over the cliff by the onrushing piano, bass and drums.

At this time Mobley was relatively inexperienced and had played in only one or two jazz combos or rhythm-and-blues bands. His front-line partner in the first Messengers band was Kenny Dorham, a trumpeter of vast skills and experience who had played in Charlie Parker's quintet and various bop aggregations over a long period of time. He would have taken the new style in his stride but Mobley may well have been almost overwhelmed by the furious rhythmic thrust of Silver, Watkins and, particularly, Blakey. It is quite conceivable that he started to devise various methods of fitting in all his phrases in an unconventional manner in order to avoid being overrun by Art, and his unusual approach to rhythm could have been created in the cauldron heated by Blakey and Silver. It is worth remembering that Hank's lack of experience had kept him out of regular jazz jobs until he linked up with the Messengers.

Michael James and many other commentators have pointed out that Mobley's original inspiration was Charlie Parker rather than the cool school pioneer, Lester Young, although in the beginning Hank's sound certainly must have taken something from Lester. The Parker connection makes much more sense when we consider that the altoist was instrumental in fashioning the most controversial and exciting rhythmic changes to jazz ever heard at this time. The ultra-advanced rhythmic ingenuity of bop was the main ingredient of the new music in the early 1940s, and when Mobley began to gain some prominence in jazz it was his rhythmic differences that most fascinated observers and followers of the music.

Along with Sonny Rollins, Hank was one of the original instigators of hard bop on the tenor saxophone, in much the same way that Dexter Gordon had translated Parker's bebop to the tenor in 1940 or thereabouts. Which is not to suggest that Rollins and Mobley were the only prime movers, just that they were the saxophonists who began to define the new style of playing, just as Blakey and Roach set the standard for drummers at the time and Silver *et al.* advanced their piano techniques in the cause. It was a new approach to bebop and gave it a prominence that far outstripped that of any other jazz style before or since, at least in terms of longevity and the number of its practitioners. Hard bop became the standard form of jazz expression round about 1956 or 1957 and continues to be the main jazz style in international use half a century later. And this is in no way intended to minimise the considerable achievements of the 'New Wave' of free jazz musicians who pioneered a collective improvisation style that was radically new in 1959–60. Ornette Coleman, Eric Dolphy, Cecil Taylor and others made significant strides towards a new style that is still in use today but on a much smaller scale both in the USA and worldwide.

To understand this we must look at what was offered by the two schools when they began. The free jazz brigade played in a manner that was often disjointed, perhaps because too much freedom inhibited them or, in some cases, outstripped their talents. Ornette Coleman, Eric Dolphy and a few others were brilliant improvisers and composers, well able to play in a new and radical style, but not every musician could handle it and there was also fierce resistance from jazz enthusiasts everywhere, which lingered for years. Even today there are many so-called jazz aficionados who cannot understand or come to terms with the music pioneered by Coleman, Don Cherry, Dolphy and Cecil Taylor and their many musical descendants.

The real enigma of Hank Mobley is that he was never really recognised as the true innovative force that he was or as a distinctive, unique tenor sax soloist. Even though jazz musicians in general and a very few jazz commentators have acknowledged his great contribution, the vast majority of the jazz community have always seen him as an outsider, rather than an innovative originator. And I believe, as will be apparent from the foregoing chapters, that he was much more of the latter than the former. So where did it all go wrong for Mobley?

Up to this point I have suggested that he was so determinedly different and unusual that he could well have alienated many of the jazz followers who took to the experimental music of Rollins and then Coltrane in the mid-1950s. And it could just be that the man who tried to do most to advance his career, Alfred Lion of Blue Note, inadvertently helped to leave him out on a limb. Mobley had more sessions left on the shelf than almost any other Blue Note regular and some of those not issued were made at a crucial time. When he was just coming up to his most productive and inventive period, earlier than most people thought, in 1957, two records showing him at a peak of his artistry, *Curtain Call* and *Poppin'*, were left on the shelf. Although he distinguished himself with *Peckin' Time*, *Soul Station*, *Roll Call* and *Workout* in 1958–61, a momentum might have come from the other two discs, plus another really excellent session; and if Lion had released together the six tracks from the 1963 date with the wonderful Herbie Hancock, Butch Warren, Philly Joe Jones rhythm section, it might just have propelled Mobley into the jazz spotlight and helped to keep him there. Speculation, of course, but a possibility surely? Careers have been built on less propitious sets of luck and circumstances.

12

Coming Home

Mobley's working sojourn in Europe lasted throughout 1968 and 1969, and he played principally in France, West Germany and Scandinavia, doing television and radio slots and, it seems, receiving an enthusiastic response from audiences wherever he appeared.

Hank decided to return home to the USA in 1970 and he should have returned to a warm welcome and continuing success. It was not to be, however, and the gradual slide downwards that marked the last years of his life really seems to have begun as early as 1970. The jazz scene was far from healthy. Straight-ahead jazz had gone into serious decline and the music was less popular than it had ever been before. Progressive rock music, the highly popular rock 'n' roll groups of the 1960s such as the Beatles, the Rolling Stones and the Beach Boys, were all in the ascendancy and, kicked off by Miles Davis and his associates, a hybrid jazz/funk music was taking centre-stage. Fusion music of all kinds was everywhere and musicians either joined its practitioners or went under; it seemed just about impossible to beat them or compete with them in any way.

Somehow Hank managed to survive, at least in the early 1970s. Although the eastern jazz scene was only a shadow of what it had been, he managed to get a gig leading a group at Slugs jazz club in New York City, where he linked up again with Cedar Walton. Some of his gigs around this time featured, along with Walton, Sam Jones on bass and Billy Higgins at the drums, sometimes with baritone saxophonist Charles Davis added to the line-up. It says much for Mobley's skill and ability as a jazz soloist and occasional leader that the Slugs engagement was a regular one that went on for a considerable time. Even when jazz was in a parlous state generally, Hank could still pack them in on live gigs.

On July 31st 1970, Mobley went into Rudy Van Gelder's studio in Englewood Cliffs to make *Thinking of Home*, which would be his last record for Blue Note. The association had lasted for sixteen years and produced many high-class albums, and nobody could have foreseen at the time that this was the end of the line. Hank had Woody Shaw on trumpet, along with Eddie Diehl on electric guitar. It was a tough rhythm section too, with Cedar Walton on piano, bassist Mickey Bass and Leroy Williams on drums. The first ten minutes of the disc were taken up with a three-part suite by Mobley with the titles – 'Thinking of Home', 'The Flight' and 'Home at Last' – indicating that he had been homesick in Europe and was, at that early stage at least, looking forward to the future in New York City.

The music on this set seems to be drenched in what Simon Spillett,[1] describes as 'resigned melancholia'. The saxophonist's tone seems softer and more resonantly mellow than on his other recordings from the period. His lines are much more in keeping with some of his late-1950s and early-1960s discs than, for example, his steely approach on recordings like *Hi Voltage* (1967) and *The Flip* (1968). Indeed, 'You Gotta Hit It' sounds like a typical Mobley hard bop opus from around 1957–58 and would not sound out of place on his *Poppin'* or *Peckin' Time* albums. It may be that Mobley was taking a look over his shoulder at past achievements and limbering up for a brighter musical future that he hoped was coming; certainly this entire set lacks the adventurousness and invention found on LPs such as *Third Season*, *A Slice of the Top* and, to a lesser extent, *Hi Voltage*. Some commentators have suggested that this is a poor record by Mobley, but the compositions and playing by the leader are, in this writer's opinion, well up to his usual high standards. It does lack some of the fire and passion of *The Flip*, recorded in Paris, and although it is rather an old-style record, the truth is that Mobley never made a bad album. He is also very well supported by Woody Shaw who, on tracks like 'You Gotta Hit It' and the final soul-type blues 'Talk About Gittin' It', actually sounds in places like late-1950s Donald Byrd.

Once again, though, Blue Note failed to issue the disc and this at a time when it would have most benefited Mobley, just returned from two years abroad and needing a new LP out on the streets for his fans to pick up on. It remained in the vaults until 1980, by which time Mobley was seldom seen or heard in public any more. Small wonder then that he was so scathing in his denunciation of Blue Note for stacking his sets on the shelf and refusing to put them out.

In 1973 Hank went to Chicago to play a weekend gig with a long-established rhythm section, pianist Muhal Richard Abrams, bassist Reggie Willis and drummer Wilbur Campbell. They played together that weekend along with trumpeter Frank Gordon and Mobley arranged to play occasional club and concert dates with the trio. As the group began to get more and more work, much of it locally, Hank made the decision to move to Chicago. A short time after he had taken up residence, local jazz writer John Litweiler managed to set up an interview with Mobley; no mean achievement as the publicity-shy saxophonist had only given a maximum of two up to that point and was to give no more during the rest of his life. But, as with Val Wilmer in London in 1968, when he *did* consent to being interviewed he seemed to have plenty to say. Maybe he felt he had to make up for all the dozens of interviews that most of his colleagues gave throughout their careers.

Of some interest to Mobley's followers who listened to and bought his records, Litweiler mentioned that the occasion of his return also meant a reunion with Arlene Lissner, a music fan from the 1950s, an assistant professor of psychiatry at the University of Illinois, and a consultant for various government health and drug abuse programmes. Litweiler asserted that by the time his article appeared in *DownBeat* magazine, Ms Lissner would be Mrs A. L. Mobley. Again, Litweiler gives us a rare glimpse into Mobley's private life, something he usually kept so quiet about. It is tempting, also, to wonder whether the couple's original meetings had more to do with psychiatry and Hank's drug abuse in the 1950s than jazz music although, possibly, it could have been a combination of both.

At the time he was living and working in Chicago and talking to John Litweiler, Hank made much of his dissatisfaction about the number of records he had recorded that were left, unissued, on the shelves. As reported in an earlier chapter he was particularly upset about the non-appearance of the music he wrote for a movie about the French–Algerian war and the recording he made with Freddie Hubbard, Cedar Walton and Curtis Fuller. He told Litweiler that he had, at that time, about five records on the shelf that Blue Note refused to put out. This seems an excessive number and rather contradicts the most usual reason that Alfred Lion used to put forward in later years, that there was so much going on at the time that some sessions were forgotten. Neither would Lion's other excuse that the sessions were not up to Blue Note standards hold water; Mobley's sets were always played to the very highest standards as even a cursory listen to any of his late-released CDs will attest. Economics seems to be the most likely explanation as it is well known that all the independent record companies were in a similar position and could only afford to put out a few records every month. If they went over their self-imposed quotas the only real option was to put LPs on the shelf for a (possible) release at a later date but many, of course, slipped through the net. Now, however, it is unlikely that we will ever know for certain why some records were held back.

'There's no point going through two, three months, trying to rehearse if they put it on the shelf,' Hank complained to Litweiler in 1973. 'I'm tired of people saying, "Do a record date." And you go through all the effort, you write something good that should be heard and they sit on it . . . What's the point of that?' Most tellingly he said: 'Blue Note had half the black musicians around New York City, and now the records are just lying around. What they do is just hold it and wait for you to die. I bet they put out all of Lee Morgan's records now.' (Morgan had died in February 1972.)

Mobley certainly had a point about the shelving of good music, although he was rather unfair to Blue Note concerning Morgan. They were one of the few companies that never tried to cash in on the death of musicians by rushing out re-releases of their music or previously unissued sessions. They concerned themselves with new music mostly and reissues or memorial albums were never timed to coincide with a musician's demise.

But Hank was already feeling somewhat pessimistic at this time and he told Litweiler that he didn't see anything in the Chicago area or the East Coast. He felt that the only alternative was California, where old friends like Benny Golson were now living and working. Neither did he have any faith in record companies or know of one he would like to record for. He complained that he couldn't find one that would give him 'leeway', and 'proper money'. And he said that he would really like to write a symphony if he could get a record company to produce it and allow him the time to rehearse it. He expressed a desire to get a government grant for his project, as he said his friends Marion Brown and Archie Shepp had done, but he did not sound as though he had much faith in the likelihood of this happening.

In answer to Litweiler's question about the records Mobley considered to be his best, he showed little faith in his own work or any preferences. Indeed, his answer suggests that he neither knew nor cared that virtually universal opinion rated the three records he made in 1960–61, starting with *Soul Station*, as his greatest recorded achievements. '*Reach Out*, *Hi Voltage*, *The Turnaround*, *A Caddy for Daddy*, they're pretty much much the same,' he replied nonchalantly. The four he mentioned, except for *The Turnaround*, were fairly recent and he may have taken little interest in his records made more than five years previously; many other jazz musicians have expressed this type of view.

It all goes to suggest, however, that Mobley, in 1973, struggling as usual to find regular work and having just had to move to an unfamiliar city to get more gigs, was already beginning to feel very low and almost despondent. The stay in Chicago did not last very long, although while there he wrote some charts for Muhal Richard Abrams, for his big band. He continued to gig with the regular rhythm section he had teamed up with but when the gigs ran out he was soon on the move once again. He was reported to have worked with Cedar Walton and Elvin Jones in 1973 but the gigs at this time seem to have been few and far between. The decline had begun.

In analysing the many possible reasons for Mobley's overall lack of acceptance, the one major factor that stands out is his refusal to publicise himself or his recordings. Talking vaguely to Litweiler about applying for a grant to write a symphony as his friends had done was useless without positive action. Lester Young had died in obscurity and was almost forgotten in 1959, after being a major contributor to the development and refinement of the tenor saxophone in jazz. To avoid a similar fate, Mobley should have put himself in the public eye more, given more interviews in the jazz press, and most importantly kept knocking on doors to try to get support and grants to rehearse and play his music. Shepp did it, and his style of jazz was hardly a commercial guarantee of public acceptance; indeed his music is largely misunderstood to this day by the jazz mainstream.

After the brief euphoria of Europe, the 1970s would be mainly downhill for Mobley with a few little sparks of success dotted throughout the early years of the decade. Together with the work with Cedar Walton and Billy Higgins, the short sojourn in Chicago seems to have been a relatively lucrative and enjoyable period. But periods of work and job satisfaction were few and far between.

Just before the Chicago move, in February 1972, he made what was to be his last LP, for the Cobblestone label. The title of the record was, ironically, *Breakthrough*, and the band was called Artistry in Music, a somewhat pretentious title although it was really the quintet he and Cedar Walton had co-led, on and off, for some considerable time. Reedman Charles Davis shared the frontline, and Sam Jones and Billy Higgins completed the rhythm section.

The music (available on CD now as 32 Jazz: 32148), like that on all his other records, gives no indication at all of the turmoil that was going on in his life at the time it was made. It does repeat a selection that he had already recorded for Blue Note on *The Flip* as 'Early Morning Stroll' and he also revisits the theme from 'The Flight' from *Thinking of Home* along with some music first heard on *Dippin'*, a record from the early 1960s. So he was still, to some extent, indulging in musical nostalgia or reliving past musical glories, as he had done on his final Blue Note album. Given everything he had gone through up to this time and the constant knocks and rebuffs and lack of sustained recognition, it is not too surprising that he retreated into repeat performances and easy music and lost the invention and originality that had always made his music so illuminating and enjoyable up to that point. No musician can be expected to go on producing great records that are fresh and personal forever, when very few people appear to be listening and few rewards are forthcoming.

This final recording, however, has plenty to recommend it. The title track 'Breakthrough' is taken very fast with Davis launching into the first solo on baritone. He sounds positively busy when compared to Mobley, who follows on with a relaxed solo that expands and varies the theme and adjusts his playing to fit all his phrases into the ultra-fast tempo, once again making it sound easy. Walton and the rhythm section drive hard, and, along with the saxophonists, provide a sound and pulse similar to that of the old Blue Note albums. If Mobley's tone is a little harder and some of his phrases a little clipped, it is probably the result of the gradual process of refinement that his style had been undergoing for the past six or seven years. Swapping choruses with Davis at the end of this track there is certainly an air of competition and Mobley, who had not recorded for over two years, was probably keen to show that he could still compete with the newer cats.

A sign of the times is the sound of Walton's electric piano at the start of 'Sabia', a relaxed line by Antonio Carlos Jobim. Mobley usually included a bossa nova or samba in his later Blue Notes and it is a safe bet that this selection was his choice. Walton takes a nicely balanced, lyrical solo here, only slightly marred by his chosen instrument, which sounds tinny. 'House on Maple Street' has a wild opening and gives the impression that we are in for a free-style outing, but it soon reverts to a loping, comfortable 4/4 and Davis solos on soprano sax. Mobley's laid-back, exploratory solo is typical of some of his early-1960s work on Blue Note and Billy Higgins has a brisk workout on the drums here. Walton has a trio feature next and plays the 'Theme from *Love Story*' with bassist and drummer in support. 'Summertime' has overtones of John Coltrane's style but virtually every modern jazz musician who played this after Trane's 1960 version seems to have been affected by it. Hank is no exception. The influence is only minor, however, as he fashions a dramatic, slow introduction that pays scant regard to the melody. Certainly there is more than enough of his unique phrasing and extemporisation in the main chorus, where he is soon working his own magic on Gershwin's classic. Indeed Walton's back-to-basics piano solo comes as something of an anti-climax.

'Early Morning Stroll' is typical hard bop and typical Hank Mobley which means, of course, that all the changes and development of his sound and style over the preceding twelve years had merely been a refining process. The basic sound and approach are the same; for all his invention and skill as an improvising soloist Mobley found a personal method of expression and kept to it for virtually the whole of his professional career. So, it is perhaps highly appropriate that the final selection on the last recording that Mobley made has him playing typical hard bop in the manner that he always played it.

As to the future, the outlook was certainly bleak at this point but, sadly, the worst was to come.

13

A Slice of the Top

There is a place in modern jazz for a music that is technically enormously sophisticated, yet retains its creator's warmth; that is as intense as the greatest contemporary works, yet presents an open, welcoming surface wherein grace, even gentle humor, appear in the stead of the conventional fierceness; that is permeated with the blues, but without sentimentality or the kind of pandering that the word 'funk' has come to represent. Hank Mobley has made that place for himself.

One of the very few regular champions of Mobley from early on in his career was John Litweiler, and the above quotation, which rather neatly encapsulates Hank's achievement to date, was written for the start of Litweiler's sleeve note to the original issue of *A Slice of the Top*. Recorded on March 8th 1966, this spirited and exciting session sat in the vaults for thirteen years, finally seeing the light of the record shop racks in 1979 when it was put out on a Liberty/United Blue Note 'Classic' LP in their LT series. Recorded by Van Gelder and produced by Alfred Lion before he left the company in the less than inspired hands of the Liberty people, it had languished, forgotten by all except Hank himself, who could get no answers to his repeated queries concerning the fate of the session.

At the time of its final, long overdue appearance, there were still five Mobley sets on the shelves, and listening to the music on *A Slice of the Top*, I was easily convinced that a good part of the responsibility for Mobley failing to make the breakthrough to public acceptance that his music deserved, must be accepted by the old Blue Note company and the executives of the new company that bought up the label in 1965. Had it appeared in 1966, along with other sterling discs from the same period that failed to appear (*Far Away Lands*, *Third Season* and Lee Morgan's *The Rajah* are prime examples of neglect) it would have given his career a boost and helped to set him up for the difficult years ahead.

He could also, of course, have benefited considerably from having another champion like Litweiler. Ira Gitler made sympathetic noises in the early 1960s with his stated surprise that the three masterworks from 1960–61 were not better received by the jazz press than they were, but this, along with Joe Goldberg's perceptive notes to *Soul Station*, were isolated incidents. The one consistent critic forever singing Hank's praises was Litweiler, who continued the notes to *A Slice of the Top* by comparing the saxophonist/composer to Beethoven, no less. Referring to H. L. Mencken's writings on Beethoven, he asserted that for both musicians there was no place for cheapness and no evasion of the artist's responsibility for immediate communication. It is also the case that although Mobley gave only a bare minimum of interviews during his career – and those at long intervals – he did talk to Litweiler more than to anybody else and the writer appears to have spoken to him before writing the sleeve note for *A Slice of the Top*.

After deploring Hank's three convictions for drug abuse, the first on a technicality, before he was in fact a user of heroin, Litweiler goes on to report that the music for this LP was conceived and written in prison, presumably in 1964, the time of his last incarceration. Lee Morgan and altoist James Spaulding complete the front line with Mobley. Hank wrote the music with Miles Davis' *Birth of the Cool* band in mind and there are obvious similarities in the way the music is scored with coloration being supplied by Howard Johnson's tuba and Kiane Zawadi's euphonium. Neither of these two low brass instruments solos, but the way their parts are written and arranged gives a distinctive and decidedly different flavour to this music. If Mobley was feeling the beginnings of despair in 1972–73, and repeating licks he had played better a thousand times before, no such stricture applies to these 1966 octet sides.

Mobley told John Litweiler that when he had finished writing this music, he handed it over to pianist/arranger Duke Pearson, the Blue Note A&R man and gave precise instructions. 'I told him I wanted the tuba to come out this way and the other instruments to come out that way,' he said and proceeded to hum the opening bars of 'A Touch of Blue' from the album. 'Duke Pearson's good with the pen,' Hank continued. 'I told him, "If I do it [write the orchestrations], I might take two weeks, but you can do it in a day."'

The full tone and the overall beauty of Mobley's sound on tenor sax is heard on *A Slice of the Top*: it is rich and abundant and the album demonstrates, in a way no other Mobley record had up to that point, how strong and individual his saxophone sound had become by the late 1960s. This is evident on all the tracks of this LP, along with the robust and harmonically rich scoring and blending of the other instruments. Mobley may be congratulated on his compositions and the way he conceived the blending together of the various voices, but a large bouquet is due to the late Duke Pearson for his imaginative arrangements.

The other striking feature of this recording is the rhythmic complexity and subtlety of Mobley's playing during his solos; he was always in the forefront of rhythmic ingenuity as a tenor soloist, but he seems to have developed it even further and even more impressively on these tracks. Litweiler's notes point out that Mobley's earlier style was built on an acute understanding of the subtleties of the rhythmic inner content and implications of Charlie Parker's phrasing. It certainly was, but although Hank lacked the supreme technical ability and boundless invention of the father of modern jazz saxophone, he managed to create his own shortcuts and knife-edged timing to create the illusion of masterful rhythmic ingenuity. Of all Hank's Blue Note records, this one gives the greatest indication of his musical methods and shows much of what he had built upon during the past sixteen years coming to fruition on a fresh and notably different type of Blue Note set. And although he claimed to have developed and refined his mature style of the 1960s by what he learned both directly from Miles Davis and indirectly from late Coltrane, the new style and burnished sound are still almost entirely Mobley. He was a true original and his description of his own playing, 'not a big sound, not a small sound, but a round sound', comes fully into focus on this disc, on *Third Season* and on some of the tracks heard on *Straight No Filter* issued in 1986.

Treading a dangerous rhythmic tightrope and managing not to fall off and hurtle down to earth was always a Mobley feature throughout his career, but it is much more pronounced on the more successful and substantial releases he recorded after 1966. If this is most obtrusive and obvious on *A Slice of the Top*, it is partly due to what John Litweiler refers to as the 'simplification of his style, for he consciously abandoned some degree of high detail in favour of concentrating his rhythmic energies. Indeed he incorporated some of Coltrane's harmonic adventures into his mature style.' Modal playing seems to have come easily to Hank, although he never really embraced it as fully as Davis and

Coltrane did in the early to late 1960s; his options were always kept open and his music embraces more than one topical method or style.

From the way the compositions in *A Slice of the Top* have been arranged and from his remarks to Litweiler it is quite obvious that Hank gave his arranger very precise instructions about what he wanted. On most of these selections, but particularly 'A Touch of Blue' and the title track of almost ten minutes, the opening ensembles are bright, robust and full of colour with the tuba, euphonium and drums very much to the fore and providing a fresh jazz sound. The approach is not like that of Gil Evans, who used the colour from tuba and French horns throughout a composition and produced a gossamer sound, like music floating on air with deftly timed punctuations from the low brass instruments. Hank's low brass, double bass and drums fairly roar out at the beginnings and endings of these tracks and set up a raging, pulsating rhythmic pulse for Mobley and Morgan to patch their solos into.

The result is something strikingly different and yet, for all that, typical Mobley; at the centre of all these pieces are sophisticated but highly personal hard bop solos with typically swinging, aggressive rhythm section backing. This is mature Mobley at his very best: his sound pure and burnished to a high degree; his rhythmic ingenuity requires knife-edged timing that he must bring off somehow, or plunge the music and his colleagues to an irrevocable stop; his inventive phrases improvise constantly, and impressively, on his own compositions. The same is true of Morgan, who often sounds as though he is using Mobley-type phrasing on these pieces, as Litweiler points out in his sleeve essay. It is a compliment to Mobley that the gifted trumpeter he more or less grew up with musically, looks to the saxophonist for inspiration and method on this record date.

So much for the two principals, but the success of this late-issued and, indeed, essential Mobley recording also owes much gratitude to the blues-based, jagged, almost 'free' excursions by James Spaulding on alto sax and some contrasting flute work, which I assume is also his as the flute is not listed on the LP personnel. McCoy Tyner also makes valuable contributions, as an accompanist in the section but more particularly as a distinctive piano soloist. Tyner, Reggie Workman on bass and Billy Higgins on drums provide a sizzling, always swinging rhythm section and it may or may not be accidental that all three were in different John Coltrane section line-ups.

Once again, though, Litweiler gets it just right as he sums up Hank's playing on *A Slice of the Top*:

> For the control and grace, the lack of belligerence in Mobley's music are deceptive; an urgent internal, very personal intensity is at the heart of his art, an all compelling involvement in which every nerve and every fibre of the imagination strain to create an ever changing web of rhythmic dares to his aggressive rhythm section.

And as Mobley himself said to the annotator when this disc first came out, 'The beat, the beat, they've got to have that beat.'

14

The Last Years

Mobley died, aged fifty-five, in Philadelphia on May 30th 1986. The official cause of death was pneumonia. Many ailments, some physical and rather more mental could be said to have been contributory causes and narcotic addiction over a long period of time could, without too much stretching of the truth, be said to embrace both. He was just as unfortunate and unlucky in death as he had been in life and, as one astute critic put it much later, even the *New York Times*, which normally notices the demise of everybody in the media or artists and musicians generally, failed to pick up on the passing of Hank Mobley, composer and tenor saxophonist extraordinary. Hank, I suspect, would just have given a wry smile and shrugged his shoulders if he could have peeped into the future before departing this life.

His last years, between his return to the USA in 1970 and his demise in 1986, had been a gradual decline into bad health and occasional bouts of depression with little in the way of public acceptance to cheer him up. There were, however, moments along the way when things went relatively well and all reports indicate that when he did play, right up to the end, he continued, characteristically, to play very well. And there were highlights occasionally. Among them were composing and arranging music for the AACM Big Band in Chicago for its leader, Muhal Richard Abrams, and working with that pianist in the sterling quintet he fronted there with the much acclaimed veteran drummer, Wilbur Campbell. Other bright spots were working with pianist and longtime friend Cedar Walton in the quintet they shared leadership of, recording his last LP for Blue Note and making his last recording of all, *Breakthrough*, for Cobblestone.

It was Walton who said of Mobley that he was 'one of the most ingenious and constantly fresh composers in modern jazz'. And this quote comes from 1980, not after Hank's death when many people appeared to find it much easier to praise his talent. Curiously, in his last years, he seems to have fared better away from New York City where he was best known and respected, at least by other musicians. As well as the successful few months in Chicago, there was a year spent in East Orange, New Jersey, close to where he was brought up and lived most of his early years, and finally a move to Philadelphia in the middle of the 1970s, where work was reported to be 'intermittent' at best.

On the down side, the 1970s saw him suffering from lung problems and he is said to have undergone two operations during this period. He also had two tenor saxophones stolen and was left with one rather beaten-up instrument that leaked badly, prompting his doctor to deliver the devastating advice that he shouldn't play it or he might blow one of his lungs out. And at the time that *A Slice of the Top* was issued he told John Litweiler that he did not have sufficient funds to buy a suitable replacement instrument. It might seem that after that it could get no worse but it did; he had long periods of inactivity in the 1970s because of his lung problems and a chance to play at a European jazz festival had to be abandoned due to what Litweiler refers to as 'a bureaucratic foul-up' with his birth certificate.

Towards the end of the 1970s Hank began to play more frequently and in more varied musical situations but, if he was working more, it was, at best, a rag bag of opportunities. He played quite often in Philadelphia bars at this period but usually as somebody's guest saxophonist or just as a result of offering to 'sit in'. He also played alto and baritone saxophones, which suggests that he was making himself available for whatever he could grab on any instrument he could play; after all, tenor sax was his chosen instrument throughout all of his recording career. Bad health continued to take its toll and severe dental problems stopped him in his tracks on many occasions. Amazingly he continued to try and find work and kept composing; at the end of the decade he had already composed over eighty songs and was still writing prolifically. It was the one musical activity that none of his misfortunes could prevent him following.

Mobley's seminal influences were the blues and Charlie Parker – the two as interchangeable and tied together as they could possibly be. His approach to jazz was soft and to some extent pretty, a Lester Young influence predominating. Young helped him develop the neat, round sound and relaxed-sounding delivery and Parker gave him the impetus to develop a predominantly blues-based approach and great rhythmic flexibility. Mobley made his debt to Parker clear when he told Litweiler in *DownBeat*:

> Where do you think everybody got the blues from? Did you ever hear 'Just Friends' and tap your foot to it? 'Soul Station' is the same thing, just like walking down the highway, it sounds like somebody saying, 'Oh man, I'm tired of this town, got to get away from this.' Parker played the modern blues; what he's saying is that so much of modern jazz, structures, harmonic progressions, they're all based on the blues.

Mobley's descriptions of what he was doing and what he felt Parker was doing are certainly couched in idiosyncratic language, obscure to anybody outside the jazz community, but to those in the know he is clearly saying, 'I'm a modern jazz musician and everything I play is inflected with the blues.' And so it was. Often, perhaps, in an oblique way; his sound shrouded in blue gauze, his tone pleading or crying with the sheer pain of those blues. And sometimes, more in happier times, he just got low down and funky and would blow the most arresting, basic and yet telling blues choruses you ever heard. 'Bass on Balls' is a good example with the ideal rhythm section of Horace Silver, Doug Watkins and Art Blakey. 'Lower Stratosphere' is another and the title tune from that masterpiece *Soul Station* is, I would suggest, the ultimate Mobley blues experience.

So when Mobley died in 1986, not many people seemed even to notice and there were few to mourn his passing. By all reports available, his last few years were tragically uneventful; he was short of money, almost destitute at times and unable to play his tenor sax for fear of seriously damaging his chronically weakened lungs. His only connection with the music scene to which he gave so much, and from which he received so little, was his continuing dedication to writing fresh music. There were even reports of a period of actual destitution where he was on the streets with no visible means of support. The most poignant words he ever spoke came long before the end. He said to John Litweiler in 1973:

> It's hard for me to think of what could be and what should have been. I lived with Charlie Parker, Bud Powell, Thelonious Monk. I walked with them up and down the street. I did not know what it meant when I listened to them cry – until it happened to me.

And by the time it happened to him, it was far too late to do anything about it. It is no easy matter trying to make a living in the precarious jazz world when you are shamefully underrated and frequently ignored by press and public, but when you can no longer play your horn, are in bad health and in financially straitened circumstances what possible hope is there? Actually, there are no real villains in this story; critics might have taken more notice and heaped more praise on Hank, but if they heard, or thought they heard, more significant music from Coltrane, Rollins, Griffin and Getz, who is to say they were wrong? And although Alfred Lion was very lax in hoarding many of Mobley's albums when release might have helped him considerably, who is to say, with conviction, that he was wrong to concentrate on the records he did put out? Mobley was by no means the only instrumentalist to suffer the annoyance of having music left in the vaults for years. The real enigma of Hank Mobley is that he somehow failed to let his considerable talent and originality shine through and was yet another victim of the jazz life.

15

Straight No Filter

In 'A Roll Call for the Round Sound', published in the October 1985 issue of *The Wire* magazine, Brian Case gave a rundown of critical descriptions of Mobley's music: Leonard Feather called him the middleweight champion of the tenor sax, John Litweiler compared him to Beethoven because there was 'no place for cheapness' in his work, and Larry Kart viewed his oeuvre as enigmatic and paradoxical. Putting his own view at the end, Case says: 'Actually, unlucky is the word that springs most readily to mind.'

Well, it's an oversimplification that has a grain of truth but I hope I have put such simple notions out of court in previous chapters. Brian Case's article, which reads like an obituary several months before Hank actually died, is symptomatic of the treatment he received over and over again from unsympathetic jazz writers. Not understanding the man and his music seems to have been an occupational hazard for some of them. Dismissing Mobley as a man who was, 'neither an innovator nor possessed of an immediately grabbing sound', Case trots out the tired old chestnut about him having the bad luck to attain the perfect expression of his gifts at a time when Coltrane and Rollins were changing the course of saxophone history.

In fact Mobley reached the peak of his creative playing powers in 1960–61, four years after Rollins turned everybody in the jazz world around with *Saxophone Colossus* and a year after Coltrane recorded *Giant Steps* and formed his ground-breaking quartet. Rollins had arguably finished making saxophone history by 1958, when he retired for two years, although Coltrane, of course, was to make history again and certainly change the course of jazz expression forever in the coming years. It is, though, typical of the way writers who should have known better dismissed Mobley or sold him grievously short on ability. Not an innovator? Not possessed of a striking tone? Many tenor saxophonists found inspiration listening to Mobley's sound and style, including Tina Brooks, Junior Cook, Frank Foster, Ronnie Scott, Tubby Hayes and many more: they would all have sung a tune different from that of Brian Case.

Making it worse and demonstrating even more clearly why Hank was so often misunderstood during his lifetime, Case goes on to suggest that Mobley's 'even urgency and serpentine lines' had more in common with Don Byas and Wardell Gray than with those of the hard bop tenor saxists. He then suggests that Hank's association with hard bop is both relevant and a red herring. This is nonsense; of course his sound was different from that of the other hard boppers – that was what made him so special – but his manner of playing the music came directly from Charlie Parker and he flourished in the admittedly more aggressive company of Horace Silver, Doug Watkins and Art Blakey, not to mention Lee Morgan, Freddie Hubbard and Philly Joe Jones. Few in jazz were more solid and committed hard boppers and few expanded the language as effectively as Hank did with his best recordings, but to some people with rigid ideas, hard bop could be played only with a fierce, jagged, ultra-hard sound and a loud, aggressive attack during solo work.

Comparing Mobley with Warne Marsh and talking about the advantages of an anonymous tone, as theorised by the Tristano school, is not helpful to anybody unfamiliar with Hank's music. Nor is suggesting that a Mobley solo requires special circumstances to come off. The magic of Mobley is that virtually all his recorded solos came off, whether he was with the Messengers, with Miles Davis, or leading the countless successful blowing sessions with Silver, Kelly, Blakey, Philly Joe Jones or Billy Higgins. His methods were unorthodox but somehow he always managed to make it work. Even teaming up with an unlikely front-line partner such as Milt Jackson on *Hank Mobley and His All Stars* in 1957 came off in spectacular fashion.

Unlucky though, yes, I'll give that one to Mr Case, because few musicians had as much bad luck as Hank. But the bad luck was compounded with misunderstanding, a self-destructive streak and, as already suggested, a desire to be original and different which went so far that it probably made a significant contribution to his downfall and early demise. Unlike that of many musicians, the Hank Mobley story does not end with his death. Consider these words by Bob Blumenthal in the liner notes for *The Complete Blue Note Hank Mobley Fifties Sessions*:

> Possessed of both his own conception, which made his music readily identifiable, and the equally rare inspiration that also made listening to his work eminently satisfying, Mobley was perpetually eclipsed throughout his career by more extroverted and influential stylists . . . When the avant-garde innovators dominated the attention of jazz critics a few years later, Mobley's playing was often dismissed as old hat and irrelevant. It has only been in the years since he stopped recording and especially since his death in 1986, that the exceptional quality of his playing and writing has begun to receive a commensurate measure of respect.

Or, to put it another way, too little, too late.

More evidence is supplied by Mobley's last record to be issued and it is not the one he made in 1972 with Cedar Walton, *Breakthrough*, but *Straight No Filter*, which came out on LP in 1986, shortly after Hank died. *Straight No Filter* offers previously unissued music from four different sessions. The first three tracks on the CD version (and they are slightly different from the tracks selected for the original LP and first CD edition) have spirited hard bop from June 17th 1966 with Lee Morgan and McCoy Tyner, both in great form, Bob Cranshaw on bass and Billy Higgins on drums. To say that these three tracks are typical of Hank's work in the 1965–67 period is almost to understate the case. The music is fast and furious, brimming over with ideas from Mobley, Morgan and Tyner and driven by a supercharged rhythm threesome.

'Chain Reaction' is the most typical hard bop opus; it moves smoothly at medium up tempo with Tyner providing the opening, smooth, flowing solo on a track that lasts just under eleven minutes. He is constantly inventive over a long, sustained solo that swings effortlessly with Cranshaw and Higgins stoking the fires behind him. Morgan's fiery, attacking trumpet solo sustains the mood and adds its own twists and turns to the narrative. Mobley enters last, relaxed as ever, his saxophone almost floating out over the rhythm section, but his solo builds urgently and very effectively in spite of his usual trick of stretching the rhythmic possibilities and yet holding the beat steady. With music of this quality it is impossible to imagine that Alfred Lion or anyone else thought it was not up to Blue Note standards.

As there are just three tracks lasting just over twenty-one minutes, it is likely that half an LP was recorded and they never managed to get together again with the same personnel to record the other three tracks needed to complete a session.

Next are two pieces from the session that produced most of *The Turnaround* with Freddie Hubbard, Barry Harris, Paul Chambers and Billy Higgins. Hubbard plays with strength and feeling, as does Mobley, and Harris proves to be, once again, an ideal pianist for Hank. Chambers and Higgins are rock solid but Chambers' bass is thinly recorded here – most unusual for Van Gelder, who normally got a first-class balance on every instrument. 'Third Time Around' is an engaging line although Hank had recorded it on other albums.

The following two tracks are from the *No Room for Squares* date in 1963, with good support from Morgan again and Andrew Hill on piano, although the latter does not always seem completely comfortable in this setting. John Ore, an underrated bassist, and the ever reliable Philly Joe Jones strike rhythmic sparks constantly. This was some of the last music to be issued with Mobley and Morgan sharing the front line and it is up to their usual high standards. Listen to 'Comin' Back' for a strong reminder of their almost telepathic compatibility.

Last and certainly best are the final two tracks taken from the magical session with Herbie Hancock on piano, Butch Warren on bass and Philly Joe Jones on drums, which should really have been issued in its entirety to make one of Mobley's finest discs. Given the creative acumen and compatibility of these musicians it is surprising that neither Blue Note nor any other record company in the 1960s ever thought to record Hancock, Warren and Jones together again.

'The Feelin's Good' has strong Mobley and a very good Donald Byrd trumpet segment but Hancock eclipses everyone with his piano solo. Sy Oliver's 'Yes Indeed' rounds off this off-beat collection of new 'old Mobley' with a bright, gospel sound generated by the springy rhythm section (listen particularly to Philly's shuffle beat) as Hank gets bluesy and bubbly. It's light and fairly frothy and certainly no masterwork. But the call and response between Mobley and Byrd is a familiar cry heard down through the years. The solos are good samples of bright blues blowing with Hank turning in an optimistic and lively segment and Byrd following in his best blues manner. Hancock's solo is the most intricate and inventive and is, perhaps, an early indication of what he could do and would go on to do.

In any event, the record is a fitting posthumous tribute to a great tenor saxophonist who should have been more widely heard and appreciated during his lifetime. More of his shelved sessions would see the light of day in the years following his death and, in the almost twenty years since then, most of his Blue Note recordings have become available or been reissued, indicating that his music is timeless, attractive to a wide-ranging jazz audience and nothing like as old-fashioned as those restricted-vision critics of the 1960s would have had us believe.

In *Jazz Journal International*, in March 2004, Simon Spillett wrote with regret about the jazz scene falling apart at the time Mobley returned to the United States from Europe because of the intrusion of 'elements foreign to the lifeblood of the mainstream of the music'. Spillett wondered, with hindsight, what might have been if Hank had decided to remain in Europe instead of returning to the country which brought about his destruction. Would he have 'eventually returned triumphant, as did his friend Dexter Gordon in the late 1970s, emerging from an acoustic jazz limbo to claim his crown as a leader of a jazz renaissance'? Well no, it isn't likely. Gordon, after all, was a jazz hero before he left America in the 1960s, had received countless plaudits from critics and observers and was an extrovert. Last, but not least, he was the owner of a big, strong, fairly aggressive sound of the kind that was fashionable throughout the 1960s and 1970s.

American writer Joe Goldberg probably got it right when he penned the liner notes to *Soul Station* in 1960:

> Hank has always been a musician's musician . . . a designation that can easily become the kiss of death for the man who holds it. Fans and critics will reel off their list of tenor players, a list that is as easily changed by fashion as not, and then the musician over in the corner will say, 'Yes, but have you heard Hank Mobley?' The musician saying that, in this particular case, might very well be a drummer. The groups Hank works in are very often led by drummers . . . Art Blakey and Max Roach to name two men who, as they say, need no introduction, and the first of whom contributes in a great degree to the success of this album.

Hank Mobley was, indeed, a musician's musician, one of a select few who appeal to virtually all other musicians but whose gifts are often obscured from the casual listener. His sound, style of playing, composing and arranging abilities were of a very high order but he failed to make a major impression on the majority of jazz critics and aficionados. He was a major stylist who never managed to make a full connection and become as big a name in jazz as Rollins, Coltrane or Getz.

16

The Legacy

On Wednesday September 25th 2002, at the Jazz Standard club in New York City, a band consisting of trumpeter Don Sickler, Branford Marsalis on tenor sax, Ronnie Mathews, piano, Peter Washington, bass, and Billy Drummond on drums played 'This I Dig of You', 'Bossa for Baby', 'Infra Rae', 'Madeline', 'East of the Village' and seven other original compositions by Hank Mobley. The next day, the same band tackled 'No Room for Squares', 'The Changing Scene', 'The Breakthrough', 'No More Goodbyes' and another twelve Mobley selections over three long sets. On the Friday, with James Williams taking over on piano, the rest of the band intact, and Eric Alexander coming in as featured tenor saxist, another eighteen of Hank's compositions were tackled including 'Workout', 'Up a Step' and 'My Groove Your Move', although one or two selections were repeats of pieces played on the other days.

This was billed as the Hank Mobley Festival and although I have no details of previous festivals it does indicate that for all his obscurity during his lifetime, a hard core of followers and admirers, both musicians and aficionados, were faithful to him and, ultimately, to his memory after he died. Ralph Moore was featured tenor saxophonist on Saturday with the usual band apart from the substitution of Mulgrew Miller at the piano. These three sets added 'Deciphering the Message', 'Greasin' Easy' and 'Dig Dis' to what had been played previously and they repeated several other favourite compositions, such as 'Soul Station' and 'East of the Village'.

The festival ended after two sets on Sunday September 29th when Cedar Walton came in on piano, appropriately as he had co-led the last combo that Hank fronted with Jimmy Greene as the featured tenor man and the usual band, they played 'The Breakthrough', 'An Aperitif', 'A Dab of This and That', 'Out of Joe's Bag' and 'No Argument'.

A tribute like this indicates that the Mobley legacy exists partly in the vast body of compositions he put together over the years (and I do mean 'put together' rather than composed, because they often were written out in the recording studios). It also shows the respect in which he was held by jazz musicians with these top soloists playing his music over a five-day festival. Although Hank's compositions were not as complex or distinctive as those of Thelonious Monk, Mobley, like that iconoclastic pianist, may well be remembered in the very long term, because of his written work.

His last appearance in public was playing with pianist Duke Jordan in 1986, shortly before he died, but the immediate and long-lasting legacy exists in the thirty-five full-length LPs he recorded as a leader, many of them available now, in one form or another, on CD. In addition there are literally dozens of records on which Hank was a featured soloist, notably the Jazz Messengers' first four LPs and definitely including *The Jazz Messengers at Café Bohemia Volumes One and Two*, *Horace Silver and the Jazz Messengers* and Horace Silver's *The Stylings of Silver*.

Also worthy of tracking down and adding to a basic collection is pianist Sonny Clark's first LP for Blue Note, *Dial S for Sonny*, available on a Connoisseur CD. Clark began his association with Blue Note in November 1957 when this session was taped and he became, over the next five years, virtually house pianist for the label before his premature death in 1963. One of Clark's best, if also one of his least known and appreciated recordings, this CD features Mobley in top form along with Art Farmer on trumpet, Wilbur Ware on bass, and Louis Hayes on drums. A very good, superior example of the Blue Note blowing date, this has some of Hank's finest early solos, played in highly compatible company. The opening title track sounds like a moody, oriental-flavoured blues and the minor theme has excellent Clark piano and Mobley tenor sax. 'Bootin' It' is also a good sampling of the early Mobley hard bop approach, the tenorist swinging hard over a fierce, driving section. 'It Could Happen to You' has superior ballad playing by Hank, Farmer and the leader.

I would certainly consider this Clark record an essential Mobley purchase and there is a bonus in buying the Connoisseur CD. It is the first stereo issue of this material and includes both the stereo and originally issued mono takes of 'Bootin' It'.

Jazz records are frequently deleted and turn up later in different guise or newly repackaged altogether, like the Jazz Factory edition that mixes Savoy sessions from 1956 with rare Debut material from 1953. Jazz buffs will always find ways of tracking down particular LPs or CDs that are desired strongly enough. I have neither the desire nor the patience to be a discographer but, out of Mobley's vast recorded output, there are certain key Mobley records that form an important part of his lasting legacy and I intend to recommend these over and above the rest. As previously indicated, I do not think that Mobley ever made a bad record and all of his discs are worthy of purchase; it is just that some are far more worthy than others.

First would be *The Hank Mobley Quartet* issued on Blue Note 5066. Hank's first quartet date, and in many ways one of his very best, was for Blue Note – a 1955 ten-inch LP – and it has been very hard to obtain over the past thirty years or so. There were alternate takes of three selections and all were included on the Mosaic set *The Complete Blue Note Hank Mobley Fifties Sessions*. Obviously this would be the best buy for anybody wanting all the music from this sterling session and all of Mobley's leader output for Blue Note from 1955 to 1958. With the high standards of mastering, an extensive booklet with photographs and essay, many alternate takes, and sessions previously available only singly in Japan, this set is very good value for money and thoroughly recommended. An alternative would be to try to get hold of secondhand LPs, again very expensive due to their rarity value, or find a source of supply for the imported Japanese CD. After those options are exhausted all you have are auctions on the internet and car boot or market sales.

After the 1955 quartet session, the next essential purchase would be the *Hank Mobley and His All Stars* set on BLP 1544. These relaxed, mainly blues or blues-related performances with Milt Jackson as the other front-line soloist and Silver, Watkins, and Blakey as the ideal rhythm section, offer some of Hank's very best playing from the 1950s. No jazz collection should be without this package, with 'Reunion', 'Lower Stratosphere' and 'Mobley's Musings' the stand-out tracks.

The disc called simply *Hank Mobley Quintet* was the last to feature the great rhythm team of Silver, Watkins and Blakey, together with Art Farmer on trumpet. Not surprisingly, this sounds like a late addition to the original Jazz Messengers sessions and it is highly recommended as another essential purchase. All the relaxation and invention typical of the original Messengers is here on the medium-tempo and ballad performances with Mobley, Silver and Farmer on great form.

Poppin' and *Curtain Call* are both very good but not, perhaps, essential. The former is readily available at the time of writing but the latter is not.

If a sampling of Hank's work for other labels is desired, the 1956 *Jazz Message of Hank Mobley Volumes One and Two* on Savoy records can be recommended. Mobley is joined here by stalwarts Donald Byrd on trumpet, Doug Watkins or Wendell Marshall on bass and Kenny Clarke or Art Taylor at the drums. Generally, though, the three Blue Note issues listed as essential will form a splendid introduction to early Mobley as a leader and function as the firm base for the beginning of a collection of his records.

The year 1960 marked Hank's greatest playing on Blue Note and the three years following produced the finest LPs of his career. *Soul Station* is, of course, his masterpiece and absolutely essential and so is the follow-up disc *Roll Call*. Both were recorded in 1960 and both featured a well nigh perfect rhythm section comprising Wynton Kelly, piano, Paul Chambers, bass, and Art Blakey, drums. Freddie Hubbard adds spicy trumpet on the later session and he too was at the peak of his creative powers at this time, as were Kelly, Chambers and Blakey.

A year later *Workout* was recorded at Rudy Van Gelder's studio with the same rhythm team except that Philly Joe Jones came in on drums and Grant Green played guitar. This disc is equally essential but another set recorded at the same time with everybody except Green on board, *Another Workout*, is not quite in the same category. It was left unissued until the 1980s even though some commentators have put it in the same league as the three classics. Readers should seek an audition and decide on that basis.

When considering essential purchases, it will be seen that the very best do not always feature Mobley as leader. Another solid classic, Kenny Dorham's *Whistle Stop* was recorded by Blue

Note in 1961 and the old front-line partnership of Mobley and Dorham cooks gorgeously. Kenny Drew, a much underrated pianist, is at the keyboard with Chambers and Jones. If you are new to jazz or new to Mobley, don't miss out on this one; add it immediately. Freddie Hubbard's *Goin' Up* is another example of Mobley at his absolute peak but working as sideman for another leader. Some, if not all, of his solos on this set are in the same quality bracket as the three acknowledged classics.

There was a gap in recording activity after 1961 but when he came back in 1963, the next Blue Note was almost in the same category as the 1960-61 material: *No Room for Squares* is certainly recommended as an essential purchase. It was, for starters, the first disc to feature two tracks with the magical Herbie Hancock, Butch Warren, Philly Joe Jones rhythm section, and the other band with Lee Morgan, Andrew Hill and Philly was smoking throughout, even though some commentators correctly pointed out that Andrew Hill was not the ideal pianist for a Mobley session.

Skip forward two years and the next essential Mobley disc was issued as *The Turnaround* with a 1965 session featuring Hank, Freddie Hubbard, Barry Harris and Paul Chambers and Billy Higgins alongside two more tracks from the Hancock, Warren and Jones date from 1963. Hank's solo style had changed, as discussed in the main text, but not enough to make LPs like these any less attractive or essential.

Between 1965 and 1968, Mobley recorded six more sets, not all of them issued at the time and none of them, in my opinion, in the same class as what had gone before. *Dippin'*, from late 1965, is probably the best but hardly an essential purchase. Discs like *Hi Voltage*, *Far Away Lands* and *A Caddy for Daddy* are all highly worthy issues although they should, I suggest, be considered for purchase only after all the essential items have been acquired. *Reach Out*, Hank's most commercial and frivolous album of them all, could safely be left to last by anybody wishing gradually to acquire all Mobley's recordings.

Third Season is a bit special and Mobley's first issued attempt at writing for and playing with a larger group. It is, I feel, a fairly essential purchase and *A Slice of the Top*, recorded slightly earlier but released much later is, as previously indicated, an absolutely essential purchase. Although both are valuable as examples of how well Mobley could write material for, and organise, a larger group of musicians, they also provide excellent examples of solo work by Mobley and, in *A Slice of the Top*, of Lee Morgan too. Both these discs should be given priority in building up a Mobley collection.

Thinking of Home was Hank's last effort for Blue Note but it is not really memorable. His penultimate Blue Note, *The Flip* is in a different category and well worth seeking out. That really completes the list, except for the posthumous release of *Straight No Filter*. This one becomes essential, not for the previously unissued 1966 session with Morgan, McCoy Tyner and Higgins but for filling up gaps with music left over from those sterling sets that produced the splendid *No Room for Squares* and *The Turnaround*. Best of all though, this disc gave us the final two selections from the March 7th 1963 date with Herbie Hancock, Butch Warren, Philly Joe and Donald Byrd, the last of the six tracks that make up the LP that never was and one of Hank's best ever, yet little-known, recording sessions.

The last session to be recorded, *Breakthrough* in February 1972, was nowhere near Hank at his very best but it does serve to remind us of his remarkable consistency and the high quality of his recorded music, right to the very end. We are fortunate that his legacy was so large and full of riches.

Epilogue

Towards the end of 2004 I went to a hotel near the British Museum in London to interview Cedar Walton for an article to be published in *Jazz Journal International*. Always a musician in great demand and a veteran of many strong Blue Note recording sessions, as well as a seasoned member of one of the classic Jazz Messenger line-ups, Cedar is one of the important links in the hard bop chain that begins around 1955–56 and continues to the present day. I was looking forward to talking to him about his career and achievements, his plans for the future and current projects but also, at the back of my mind, lurked the thought that if anybody could throw light on the silence that seems to surround Hank Mobley's final years, Cedar was the man to provide it. He was, after all, one of the last musicians to play regularly with Hank and had been co-leader on Mobley's last album: *Breakthrough*. It had been pointed out to me that Mobley's last few years were almost a complete mystery and for the sake of thoroughness (not to mention tidiness) I needed to try and unravel what had happened during that final period.

Walton is a very easy person to talk to, open, eager to discuss the music and his fellow musicians and with seldom a bad word to say about anybody. But even he was unable to throw much light on Mobley's final days. When we finally got round to the subject I mentioned that Cedar had worked with Hank in the 1980s and that they had recorded together for Cobblestone Records in 1972 on a set that turned out to be Hank's last ever on record.

'Yes,' said Cedar, 'for that session we were co-leaders on record but for the most part Hank was a leader on his own when he played. He was another friendly sort, like Coltrane, soft-spoken and, as I say, a prolific composer in jazz.'

And, I asked, a great soloist?

'Oh yes, I totally agree. An original style that had great softness, warmth and a complete command of that language.'

But why were his last years shrouded in mystery?

'Well, the thing is, he moved out to Philadelphia and wasn't as visible during his last years. He did not play in New York at all. I do remember playing in several concerts there titled *Tribute to Hank Mobley*.'

Walton knew very little about those final months. He had had scant contact with Mobley at that time but he did recall a concert where he had played with Hank under trumpeter Kenny Dorham's leadership:

> a one-off gig at a place in Harlem called the Armoury. A huge place, as most armouries are. They had a big West Indian band and then we came on and I could see Hank making his way through the crowd and we had already started the song and Hank just got up on stage and put the horn in his mouth just in time to start his solo. I thought this was unique and typically Hank. He arrived right on the beat; there was a big crowd, all standing up, It was a type of dance hall.

Cedar felt that Mobley was a proud man who went into hiding at the end:

> I just think that with the amount of pride he had, he hid out. I call it hiding out. He decided to relocate in Philadelphia which is much less visible. And there he could eventually play in bars where he was not so well known.

That is certainly part of it and Cedar was keen to help further but unable to do so; he suggested that I get in touch with trumpeter/arranger Don Sickler in the USA who, he said, 'was closer to Hank at the end than anybody else'. When Walton's tenor saxophonist on the tour came into the bar where we were talking, he also suggested Sickler as the most likely person to shed light on Hank's final months. I emailed veteran American jazz authority and writer Ira Gitler who replied promptly to my request for information but he too said that he had little or no contact with Mobley during his final years in Philadelphia. He did, however, suggest that I contact Don Sickler so Sickler became the man I was most anxious to communicate with. Progress? Not really. All attempts to make contact with him have failed; after several emails, and a letter by old-fashioned post, I am forced to conclude that either he does not wish to discuss Hank's last years, perhaps because it is too painful, or maybe he is simply too busy. Dead end looming.

Another friend, a jazz pianist, suggested that I contact British tenor saxophonist Renato D'Aiello, who is known to be a great admirer of Mobley so I sent him an email. He replied, saying that he could not help personally but recommended that I contact a tenor saxist in America who 'may be helpful', Andy Farber. I wrote to him but, once again, no reply. Either there is a conspiracy of silence on the subject of Hank's last years or nobody knows anything and they have little time or inclination to discuss it. Maybe there just isn't anything else to know.

In death, as in life, Hank Mobley remains an enigma. An exhaustive search of the internet for any other possible clues or information that might be out there again came up with nothing. There is really no way of knowing for sure, at the time of writing, but pianist Cedar Walton may have been nearest to the mark when he suspected that Hank just 'went into hiding'. And if that was the case then it is entirely likely and laudable that close friends and close musical associates who may be in the know would want to respect his wishes and his desire for privacy and say nothing about his activities during his final weeks.

Hank Mobley has gone but his music is out there, on his many recordings, for us to listen to and enjoy. That is his true legacy. The rest is rumour and speculation and may well remain so. It is certainly the case that at the time of writing, Mobley's recordings, on CD (and even on limited-edition LPs now that there is something of a vinyl revival going on), are almost all available and in print. Hank is far more popular and respected than he ever was in his lifetime. Unfortunately it can no longer do him any good, but his great, idiosyncratic and so personal music is at least out there and available for everybody to enjoy. The music the man made, the joy in much of his playing and the uniqueness of his approach and sound, are a cause for celebration that he was so successful in the most important aspect of his career; his music making and writing. His compositions will be played at jazz clubs and concerts for as long as jazz music is performed. And his records are going to be played for as long as there is a format for reproducing them.

Notes

Chapter One *Early Messages*
1. John Litweiler, 'The Integrity of the Artist – the Soul of the Man', *DownBeat*, March 29th 1973.
2. Larry Kart, sleeve notes to Blue Note GXF 3066 (Japan).
3. Bob Blumenthal, sleeve notes to Mosaic MD6–181.
4. Alyn Shipton, *A New History of Jazz* (London: Continuum, 2001) p.679.
5. Richard Cook and Brian Morton, *The Penguin Guide to Jazz on CD*, fourth edition (London: Penguin Books, 1998).
6. Bob Blumenthal, sleeve notes to Blue Note 32148-2 and 32149-20.

Chapter Two *A Leader on Records*
1. Bob Blumenthal sleeve notes to BLP 75339.
2. Bob Blumenthal, sleeve notes to Mosaic MD6-181.

Chapter Four *The Jazz Life*
1. John Litweiler, 'The Integrity of the Artist – the Soul of the Man', *DownBeat* March 29th 1973.
2. Robert Levin, sleeve notes to Blue Note 1550.
3. J. C. Thomas, *Chasin' the Trane – The Music and Mystique of John Coltrane* (London: Elm Tree Books, 1976).
4. John Litweiler, as above.

Chapter Five *Poppin' and the Curtain Call Sessions*
1. Nat Hentoff, sleeve notes to Blue Note LP 84425.
2. Larry Kart, sleeve notes to GXF 3066.

Chapter Six *Soul Station*
1. Max Harrison *et al.*, *Modern Jazz – The Essential Records* (London: Aquarius Books, 1978).

2. Joe Goldberg, sleeve notes to BLP 4034.
3. Robert Levin, sleeve notes to Blue Note CDP 7 46823 2.

Chapter Seven *Working Out*
1. Sleeve notes to Sony/Columbia Legacy CK65919.
2. John Szwed, *So What: The Life of Miles Davis* (London: William Heinemann, 2002).
3. Miles Davis with Quincy Troupe, *Miles, the Autobiography* (London: Macmillan, 1989).
4. *Jazz Journal International*, March 2004.
5. Miles Davis, *Friday & Saturday Nights at the Black Hawk*, Complete Sony/Columbia Legacy, C2K 87097 and C2K 87100.

Chapter Eight *The Turnaround*
1. John Litweiler, 'The Integrity of the Artist – the Soul of the Man', *Down Beat* March 29th 1973.
2. *DownBeat*, August 16th 1961.
3. John Litweiler, as above.
4. Leonard Feather, sleeve notes to Blue Note 84080.
5. Del Shields, sleeve notes to Blue Note 84186.

Chapter Nine *Consolidation*
1. Ronald Atkins, review of Eric Dolphy's *Out to Lunch* in Max Harrison, *Modern Jazz: The Essential Records* (London: Centurion Books, 1975, p.112).
2. Ira Gitler, sleeve notes to Blue Note 84230.
3. John Litweiler, sleeve notes to Blue Note 97506.
4. *Jazz Spotlight News*, Volume 2, No. 1, Summer 1980 and John Litweiler, *Down Beat*, March 29th 1973.

Chapter Ten *Europe*
1. Dave Gelly, 'Terse Tenor', *Jazz Journal*, September 1986, p.112.
2. Val Wilmer, 'Daddy of the Hard Bop Tenor', *Melody Maker*, May 11th 1968.
3. Bob Dawbarn, *Melody Maker*, May 25th 1968.
4. Leonard Feather sleeve notes to Blue Note 84329.

Chapter Eleven *The Enigma of Hank Mobley*
1. Michael James, 'Hank Mobley', *Jazz Monthly*, October 1961.

Chapter Twelve *Coming Home*
1. Simon Spillett, 'Hank Mobley in Europe 1968–70', *Jazz Journal International*, January 2004.

Records

CD issues come and go and have different catalogue numbers with each new re-release. The classic Blue Note and Savoy issues are known by their original numbers and specialist jazz record shops can always advise and often track down the latest CDs from these. At the time of writing all the listed records are available on CD in various forms or with additional tracks. For example, Doug Watkins' Transition 20 album *Watkins at Large* is available as a Blue Note double CD (listed below), a Japanese CD on both Transition and Blue Note and as a 200 gram vinyl LP from Classic Records in USA. The listing below is not complete but covers the music referred to in this book.

Max Roach Quartet 1953 OJC 202 CD

Hank Mobley Quartet 1955 Blue Note 5066 LP 10-inch & CD (available on CD only on Mosaic box set or Japanese import)

Horace Silver and the Jazz Messengers 1954/55 Blue Note 1518

The Jazz Messengers at Café Bohemia 1955 Blue Note 1507/8 (2)

Donald Byrd Sextet *Byrd's Eye View* 1955 Transition TRLP 4

Hank Mobley Quintet 1956 Savoy MG 12092

Introducing Lee Morgan, with the Hank Mobley Quintet 1956 Savoy MG 12091

The Prestige All Stars 1956 Prestige 7074

Horace Silver Quintet *Six Pieces of Silver* 1956 Blue Note 1539

Hank Mobley Sextet 1956 Blue Note 1540

Lee Morgan Sextet *Lee Morgan Volume 2* 1956 Blue Note 1541

Doug Watkins Sextet *Watkins at Large* 1956 Transition TRLP 20. (This session and TRLP 4 (above) are available on Blue Note 40528 *The Transition Sessions* 2 CDs)

Hank Mobley Quintet *Hank Mobley and His All Stars* 1957 Blue Note 1544

Hank Mobley Quintet 1957 Blue Note 1550

Johnny Griffin Septet 1957 Blue Note 1559

Sonny Clark Quintet *Dial S for Sonny* 1957 Blue Note 1570

Hank Mobley Sextet *Hank* 1957 Blue Note 1560

Horace Silver Quintet 1957 Blue Note 1562

Hank Mobley Sextet *Hank Mobley* 1957 Blue Note 1568

Hank Mobley Quintet 1957 Blue Note BNJ 61006 (Japan only, as a single CD or LP)

Hank Mobley Sextet 1957 Blue Note GFX 3066 (Also Japan only)

Hank Mobley / Lee Morgan Quintet 1958 Blue Note 1574

Art Blakey and the Jazz Messengers *At the Jazz Corner of the World Volumes 1 & 2* 1959 Blue Note 4015/4016

Dizzy Reece Quintet *Starbright* 1959 Blue Note 4023

The Complete Blue Note Hank Mobley Fifties Sessions, 1956–1959 6 CD box set Mosaic MD6-181

Hank Mobley Quartet *Soul Station* 1960 Blue Note 4031

Freddie Hubbard Quintet *Goin' Up* 1960 Blue Note 4056

Hank Mobley Quintet *Roll Call* 1960 Blue Note 4058

Kenny Dorham Quintet *Whistle Stop* 1961 Blue Note 4063

Philly Joe Jones / Elvin Jones Septet 1961 *Together* Atlantic 1428

Miles Davis *Someday My Prince Will Come* 1961 Columbia CL 1656

Hank Mobley Quintet *Workout* 1961 Blue Note 4080

Hank Mobley *Another Workout* 1961 Blue Note 84431

Miles Davis Quintet *In Person – Friday and Saturday Nights at the Blackhawk, San Francisco* 1961 Columbia 1669/1670 2 LPs

Hank Mobley Quintet *No Room for Squares* 1963 Blue Note 4149

Hank Mobley Quintet *The Turnaround* 1965 Blue Note 4186

Hank Mobley Quintet *Dippin'* 1965 Blue Note 4209

Hank Mobley Sextet *A Caddy for Daddy* 1965 Blue Note 4230

Hank Mobley Octet *A Slice of the Top* 1966 Blue Note LT 995

Hank Mobley Quintct *Straight No Filter* 1963/66/68 Blue Note 84435

Lee Morgan Quintet *The Rajah* 1966 Blue Note 84426

Hank Mobley Septet *Third Season* 1967 Blue Note LT 1081

Hank Mobley Quintet *Far Away Lands* 1967 Blue Note 84425

Hank Mobley Sextet *Hi Voltage* 1967 Blue Note 84273

Hank Mobley Sextet *Reach Out* 1968 Blue Note 84288

Hank Mobley Sextet *The Flip* 1969 Blue Note 84329

Hank Mobley Sextet *Thinking of Home* 1970 Blue Note LT 1045

Cedar Walton / Hank Mobley Quintet *Breakthrough* 1972 Cobblestone CST 9011/Muse MR 513

Index

Abrams, Muhal Richard, 127, 130, 141
Adams, Pepper, 10, 42
Adderley, Cannonball, 64
Alexander, Eric, 152
Ammons, Albert, 16
Ammons, Gene, 35
Anderson, Cat, 7
Armstrong, Louis, xi, 48
Artistry in Music, 131
Atkins, Ronald, 90, 170
Atlantic Records, 45, 49, 58, 73, 110
Ayler, Albert, 2
Baker, Chet, 40
Barkan, Todd, 126
Bass, Mickey, 126
Beach Boys, the, 125
Beatles, the, 125
Bechet, Sidney, 15
Beethoven, Ludwig Van, 135, 145
Beiderbecke, Bix, xi
Benedetti, Vince, 111
Bennett, Tony, 87
Benson, George, 99
Berlin, Irving, 33, 48
Bethlehem Records, 82
Birdland, New York, 12-13, 18, 54
Black Hawk, San Francisco, 64, 68-9, 71-3
Blakey, Art, 7-14, 18, 20, 23, 27, 33, 37, 44, 46, 49-50, 54-6, 66, 91, 97, 107, 122, 119, 121-2, 143, 150-1, 155, 160-1
Blue Note Records, ix, 2-3, 8, 11, 15-16, 19-21, 25-9, 31, 33, 35, 38-50, 54-5, 58-61, 63, 66, 69, 73-6, 79-80, 82-3, 86-7, 89-91, 93-4, 97, 105, 108, 110-112, 115, 123, 126-9, 131-7, 141, 147-50, 153-9
Blumenthal, Bob, 11, 14, 22-3, 147, 163
Booker, Walter, 97, 108, 111
Brooks, Tina, 27, 146
Brown, Clifford, 7, 12, 16, 21, 38, 40, 55, 74, 121
Brown, Marion, 130
Burrell, Kenny, 27
Byas, Don, 5, 101-2, 112, 115, 150
Byrd, Donald, 11, 15, 20-1, 26-8, 39-40, 63, 75, 82, 87, 97, 120, 127, 149-50, 156, 158
Café Bohemia, New York, 9, 11-14, 26, 45, 153
Campbell, Wilbur, 127, 141
Carnegie Hall, New York, 69, 71-2
Carney, Harry, 7
Carter, Ron, 64, 67, 69
Case, Brian, 145-7
Chambers, Paul, 21-2, 34, 37, 42-3, 46, 50, 55, 57-9, 63-4, 72-3, 86, 95, 108, 111, 119, 149, 156-7
Cherry, Don, 123
Clark, Sonny, 34, 39-42, 111, 153-4
Clarke, Kenny, 28, 30, 101-2, 109, 156
Club 43, Manchester, 109
Cobb, Jimmy, 57, 64, 78
Cobblestone Records, 131, 141, 159
Cohn, Al, 19
Coleman, Ornette, x, xi, 10, 76, 109, 122, 123

Colomby, Harry, 32
Coltrane, John, ix-xi, 1, 10, 13, 19, 34-40, 42, 48-9, 51, 57, 62-8, 70-1, 76, 78, 81, 84-5, 94, 104, 115-6, 123, 133, 137, 138-9, 144-6, 151, 160
Columbia Records, 20, 25, 71-3
Comegys, Leon, 28
Connoisseur Records, 153-4
Contemporary Records, 38
Cook, Junior, 146
Cook, Richard, 14, 163
Cook, Willie, 7
Cranshaw, Bob, 59, 94, 99, 111, 148
Cullaz, Alby, 111
Cuscuna, Michael, viii, 27, 81
D'Aiello, Renato, 161
Dameron, Tadd, 7
Davis, Charles, 126
Davis, Miles, 5, 10, 19, 38, 40, 48, 51, 57-60, 62-73, 76, 79-81, 84, 91, 97, 115-7, 125, 132-3, 136-7, 147, 164
Davis, Walter, Jr., 5, 28-9
Dawbarn, Bob, 107, 164
Debut Records, 28, 30, 154
Distel, Sacha, 87
Dolphy, Eric, x-xi, 78, 122-3, 164
Dorham, Kenny, 6-8, 10-11, 14-16, 18, 26, 32-3, 40-1, 46, 69, 73-8, 82, 102, 115, 121, 156-7, 160
DownBeat, 4, 52, 56, 76-7, 83, 128, 142, 163-4
Drew, Kenny, 58, 69, 73, 78, 113-14, 119, 157
Drummond, Billy, 152
Edgehill, Arthur, 7-8
Ellington, Duke, 6
Esquire Records, 45
Evans, Bill, 64
Evans, Gil, 66, 71-2, 142

Farber, Andy, 161
Farmer, Art, 10, 32-3, 40, 42, 154-5
Feather, Leonard, 21-2, 60, 85, 112, 145, 164
Ferreira, Djalma, 93
Five Spot Cafe, 3, 103
Foster, Frank, 146
Freeloader, Freddie, 91
Fuller, Curtis, 59, 73, 94, 128
Garland, Red, 64
Gayten, Paul, 5, 7
Gelly, Dave, 3, 52, 91, 103, 164
Gershwin, George, 133
Getz, Stan, x, 9-10, 85, 107, 120, 144, 151
Gillespie, Dizzy, x-xi, 7, 21, 40, 55, 97, 121
Gitler, Ira, 83-4, 90, 93-5, 135, 161, 164
Goldberg, Joe, 49-51, 81, 135, 151, 163
Golson, Benny, 129
Gonsalves, Paul, 7, 101
Gordon, Dexter, 5, 102, 109, 113, 117, 122, 150
Gordon, Frank, 127
Gordon, Joe, 14, 26-7
Green, Grant, 60-1, 74, 156
Greenwich, Sonny, 96
Griffin, Johnny, x, 13, 35-7, 101-2, 144, 178
Gryce, Gigi, 28
Hall, Edmond, 15
Hamilton, Jimmy, 6
Hampton, Lionel, 77, 111
Hampton, Slide, 100, 110
Hancock, Herbie, 64, 69, 73, 79-80, 82, 87, 124, 149, 157-8
Hannan, Tom, 25
Harris, Barry, 3, 86-7, 111, 149, 157
Harrison, Max, 163-4

Hawkins, Coleman, x-xi, 1, 9, 51, 79, 85
Hayes, Tubby, 107, 146
Heath, Al 'Tootie', 113
Heath, Jimmy, 62
Henderson, Eddie, 63-4, 66, 69
Hennessey, Mike, 177-8
Hentoff, Nat, 39, 99, 163
Hicks, John, 108, 119
Higgins, Billy, 59, 86-7, 90, 93-6, 99, 102, 108, 119, 126, 133, 139, 147-9, 157-8
Hill, Andrew, 80-1, 149, 157
Holiday, Billie, 5
Hope, Elmo, 35
Howard Theatre, Washington, 62
Hubbard, Freddie, 55-60, 69, 73-5, 77, 82, 86-7, 102, 108, 128, 146, 149, 156-7
It Club, Los Angeles, 94
Jackson, Milt, 23-4, 41, 147, 155
James, Michael, 47, 118-21, 165
Jazz Door Records, viii
Jazz Factory, 28-30, 154
Jazz Journal, viii, 3, 47, 53, 65, 150, 159, 164-5
Jazz Messengers, 7-14, 18, 20, 23, 26-7, 32-4, 39-41, 44-5, 50, 54, 63, 66, 69, 76, 91, 107, 121, 147, 153, 155, 159
Jazz Monthly, viii, 120, 165
Jazz Prophets, 14
Jazzhus Montmartre, Copenhagen, 119
Jenkins, John, 40
Jobim, Antonio Carlos, 132
Johnson, Howard, 136
Johnson, J. J., 70
Johnson, Lamont, 99
Jones, Elvin, 58, 63, 73-4, 90, 130

Jones, Philly Joe, 34, 40, 42, 44, 46, 57-60, 63-4, 67, 73-5, 79-83, 108-13, 119, 124, 146-7, 149, 156-8
Jones, Sam, 126
Jones, Thad, 27
Jordan, Cliff, 39
Jordan, Duke, 27, 153
Joyner, George, 40
Kamuca, Richie, 9
Karloff, Boris, 58
Kart, Larry, 10, 43, 145, 163
Kelly, Wynton, 37, 43, 46, 50, 55, 58-60, 63-4, 69, 72-4, 111, 119, 147, 156
King, Pete, 107, 109
Koenig, Les, 38
Konitz, Lee, 70
Kotick, Teddy, 39
Land, Harold, 7
Le Chat-qui-Pêche, Paris, 109
Levin, Robert, 32, 56, 163
Levin, Tony, 107
Liberty Records, 59, 110, 134
Lion, Alfred, 2, 11, 15-16, 20, 25, 42, 56, 58-9, 79-80, 82, 85-6, 110, 123, 128, 134, 144, 148
Lissner, Arlene, 128
Litweiler, John, viii, 4-7, 15, 31, 34-6, 57, 59, 76, 79-81, 96, 100-1, 127-30, 134-9, 141-3, 145, 163-4
London Records, 45
Lovette, Harold, 58
Mabern, Harold, 94-5
Macero, Teo, 71-2
Marsalis, Branford, 152
Marsh, Warne, 70, 147
Marshall, Wendell, 156
Massey, Cal, 95
Mathews, Ronnie, 152
Mathewson, Ronnie, 107
McBee, Cecil, 108

McLean, Jackie, 6, 34, 89, 93, 97, 102, 105, 108
Melody Maker, viii, 92, 100, 164
Mencken, H. L., 135
Miles, Reid, 25
Miller, Mulgrew, 153
Mingus, Charles, 28
Minton's Playhouse, New York, 7
Mitchell, Blue, 73
Mobley, Dave, 5-6
Monk, Thelonious, x-xi, 16, 55, 115, 143, 153
Montgomery, Wes, 60
Montmartre Club, Copenhagen, 113
Moore, Brew, 113
Moore, Ralph, 152
Morgan, Lee, 21-2, 37, 44-5, 54-5, 61, 63, 74-5, 80, 82-3, 86, 89-95, 102, 108, 119, 129, 135, 138, 146, 148-9, 157-8
Morton, Brain, 14
Morton, Brian, 163
Mosaic Records, vii, 11, 22-3, 39, 155, 163
Mulligan, Gerry, 6
Nance, Ray, 7
Navarro, Fats, 16, 40, 55
New York Times, 140
Oliver, Sy, 149
Ore, John, 80-1, 83, 149
Original Dixieland Jazz Band, 77
Pacific Jazz Records, 45
Parker, Charlie, x-xi, 6, 9, 26, 29, 31, 34, 48, 52, 85, 121-2, 137, 142-3, 146
Pearson, Duke, 96, 136
Pedersen, Niels-Henning Ørsted, 113, 116
Perkins, Bill, 9
Persip, Charli, 21-2, 44

Pettiford, Oscar, 6
Porter, Cole, 10, 33
Powell, Bud, 5, 16, 104, 147
Prestige Records, 2, 15, 19-20, 28, 35, 45, 75, 82, 94
Pyne, Mike, 107
Quebec, Ike, 41
Reece, Dizzy, 73, 110-12
Reinhardt, Django, 77
Ridley, Larry, 93
Rivers, Larry, 90
Rivers, Sam, 62
Riverside Records, 38
Roach, Max, 2, 6-7, 12, 28-29, 38-9, 121-2, 151
Rolling Stones, 125
Rollins, Sonny, ix-xi, 1, 6-7, 9, 13, 16, 28, 31, 34, 38-40, 42, 48, 51, 53, 66, 70, 84, 104, 115, 122-3, 144-6, 151
Ronnie Scott's Club, London, 97, 106-7, 109
Roulette Records, 2
Rowser, Jimmy, 40-1
Savoy Records, 2, 15, 19-20, 28-30, 44, 48, 75, 82, 154, 156
Scott, Ronnie, 47, 97, 106-7, 109, 146
Shaw, Woody, 99, 126-7
Shepp, Archie, 101, 105, 112, 130
Shields, Del, 86, 88, 164
Shipton, Alyn, 13, 163
Shorter, Wayne, 64-5, 67, 69, 95, 107
Sickler, Don, 157, 160-1
Silver, Horace, 7-11, 13-14, 16, 18, 20-1, 27, 33-4, 39, 41, 63, 66, 76, 93, 108, 119, 121-2, 143, 146-7, 153, 155
Sims, Zoot, 9, 19
Skeete, Franklin, 29

Slugs club, New York, 90, 92, 126
Smith, Jimmy, 16, 108
Sony record company, 25, 68, 71
Spaulding, James, 98, 143
Spillett, Simon, 47, 65-6, 126, 150, 165
Stitt, Sonny, 5, 35, 62
Sulieman, Idrees, 28
Szwed, John, 64, 66, 69, 170
Taylor, Art, 27, 40-1, 101, 119, 156
Taylor, Cecil, x, xi, 78, 122-3
Taylor, Ian Scott, 111
Thomas, J. C., 35, 163
Thompson, Lucky, 107
Timmons, Bobby, 34, 40, 45, 54
Tiomkin, Dmitri, 27
Tolliver, Charles, 108
Transition Records, 14, 25-7, 30
Troupe, Quincy, 65
Tyner, McCoy, 74-5, 94, 111, 139, 148, 158
United Artists Records, 25
Van Gelder, Rudy, 3, 11-16, 20, 23, 30-1, 46, 55, 76, 93, 99, 126, 134, 149, 156
Vogue Records, 45
Walton, Cedar, 59, 63, 90, 95-6, 102, 108, 111, 119, 126, 130-3, 141, 148, 153, 159-61
Ware, Wilbur, 40, 154
Warren, Butch, 79-80, 82-3, 127, 149, 157-8
Washington, Peter, 152
Watkins, Doug, 7-8, 11, 20, 23, 26-8, 32-4, 39, 119, 121, 146, 155-6
Webster, Ben, 29, 109, 113
Weinstock, Bob, 19
Williams, James, 152
Williams, Leroy, 126
Williams, Tony, 64, 67
Willis, Reggie, 127

Wilmer, Val, 92, 102-5, 108-9, 118, 128, 164
Wilson, John S., 76
Wilson, Tom, 25, 77
Wire, The, 145
Wolff, Francis, ix, 15-16, 20, 25, 110
Woods, Phil, 110
Workman, Reggie, 139
Young, Lester, x-xi, 1, 5, 9-10, 13, 19, 29, 39-40, 51, 66, 79, 85, 120, 122, 131, 142
Zawadi, Kiane, 136

JAZZ BOOKS FROM NORTHWAY

John Chilton
Hot Jazz, Warm Feet

Vic Ash
I Blew It My Way: Bebop, Big Bands and Sinatra

Alan Plater *Doggin' Around*

Ronnie Scott with Mike Hennessey
Some of My Best Friends Are Blues

Ron Brown with Digby Fairweather
Nat Gonella — A Life in Jazz

Peter Vacher
Soloists and Sidemen: American Jazz Stories

Alan Robertson
Joe Harriott — Fire in His Soul

Coleridge Goode and Roger Cotterrell
Bass Lines: A Life in Jazz

Digby Fairweather
Notes from a Jazz Life

Harry Gold
Gold, Doubloons and Pieces of Eight

Jim Godbolt
A History of Jazz in Britain 1919–50

Jim Godbolt
All This and Many a Dog

Ian Carr
Music Outside

FORTHCOMING JAZZ BOOKS FROM NORTHWAY

Mike Hennessey
The Little Giant: Johnny Griffin

Chris Searle
*Forward Groove: Jazz and the Real World
from Louis Armstrong to Gilad Atzmon*

Graham Collier
The Jazz Composer – Moving Music off the Paper

Peter King
an autobiography

Ron Rubin
musical limericks

www.northwaybooks.com